TEARS AND SAINTS

TEARS
AND
SAINTS

E. M. CIORAN

Translated and with an Introduction by
ILINCA ZARIFOPOL-JOHNSTON

The University of Chicago Press ✧ *Chicago and London*

E. M. CIORAN was born and educated in Romania and has
lived in Paris since 1937. He is the author of numerous works, several of which have appeared in English, including *On the Heights of
Despair,* published by the University of Chicago Press in 1992.

ILINCA ZARIFOPOL-JOHNSTON, a Romanian na-
tive, is associate professor of comparative literature at Indiana
University. She has also translated Cioran's *On the Heights of Despair.*

The University of Chicago Press, Chicago 60637
The University of Chicago Press, Ltd., London
©1995 by The University of Chicago
All rights reserved. Published 1995
Printed in the United States of America
04 03 02 01 00 99 98 97 96 95   1 2 3 4 5
ISBN: 0–226–10672–1 (cloth)

Library of Congress Cataloging-in-Publication Data

Cioran, E. M. (Emile M.), 1911–
    [Lacrimi şi sfinţi. English]
    Tears and saints / E. M. Cioran ; translated by Ilinca Zarifopol-
Johnston.
        p.   cm.
    Includes bibliographical reference.
    1. Suffering.   2. Christian saints—Miscellanea.   I. Title.
B105.S79C56   1995
235′.2—dc20   95-13187

Title page illustration: detail from *The Descent from the Cross*, Rogier van
der Weyden. Photograph copyright Museo del Prado, Madrid. All rights
reserved. Partial or total reproduction prohibited.

INTRODUCTION

Cioran: The Temptation to Believe

The "death of the author" is a notion I have never become used to. Time and again, when I open the pages of an engaging book, the "dead" author comes back to haunt me: as if reading were a spell that brings him back, his hovering spirit is always before my mind's eye. And while reading, the desire to capture this spirit, to know him, "to be *him*" takes possession of me. I cannot read without imagining the "dead" author back to life.

E. M. Cioran is an author that wants imagining more than others. As a writer, he is particularly well versed in the game of making and unmaking authorial fictions in his texts, a game complicated by the fact that in real life he has had two lives, two identities, two authorial voices: the Romanian Cioran of the 1930s and the French Cioran—much better known—of the 1970s and

1980s. I began imagining Cioran when I translated his first Romanian book, *On the Heights of Despair* (Bucharest, 1934; University of Chicago Press, 1991). Now, having translated another of his Romanian books, *Tears and Saints*, published in Bucharest in 1937 shortly after he had left Romania for Paris never to return, I find myself again caught up in the skein of imagination, while the tantalizing question endures: Who is this man?

Erased from history as a nonperson in Communist Romania, little known in the West outside elite intellectual circles, Cioran eludes me yet again in his final tragic illness. This master of style can speak now only with his eyes. There is a cruel poetic justice in this, for the mystical experience he meditated on in *Tears and Saints* places great emphasis on the eye, on seeing the invisible, on acquiring intimate knowledge of a different, nonempirical reality. Since the very notion of a mystical language is paradoxical—only silence can encompass the infinite and the invisible—it may be appropriate that Cioran should now be silent, or speak with his eyes. Like his saints, Cioran is now wholly an outsider. He has always been one in various ways, but his transition to another "twilight zone" is now total and irrevocable. His intense green eyes are like pools of otherworldly luminosity. I looked into them last summer as I told him about my detective work on his saints, how hard it was to track some of them down—some, in fact, I never did. I wanted to know why he had chosen such a recondite subject to write about. Lately, saints and angels have become quite fashionable, but I couldn't help wondering whether there was anyone in the 1930s as familiar with these saintly figures as Cioran was. He listened to me as if from afar, his eyes lit up with amused mischief, his lips sealed. Cioran has already removed himself from this world of confusion, leaving in our hands the multi-colored coat of his writings to puzzle over. My author is not dead, he has only made his escape into another world, and there he lives to tantalize his reader, to tease, to challenge, to spur her on. Henceforth I shall follow him, the reader in search of the author. Where will I find him first?

Romania, mid-1930s. A passionate young man, already known as a flamboyant writer in a new generation of intellectuals, Cioran spends hours in a Transylvanian library in his hometown, Sibiu, poring over the lives of saints. A modern-day hagiographer, he has "dreamt" himself "the chronicler of these [saints'] falls between heaven and earth, the intimate knower of the ardors in their hearts, the historian of God's insomniacs." The question naturally arises: why would a healthy, normal young man, who confesses his love of life openly, who is politically active, want to become a "heavenly inter-loper" spying on the saints' secrets? A partial answer may be found in a passage from Nietzsche's *Beyond Good and Evil:*

> The mightiest men have hitherto always bowed re-verently before the saint, as the enigma of self-subjugation and utter voluntary privation—why did they thus bow? They divined in him . . . the superior force which wished to test itself by such a subjugation; the strength of will, in which they recognized their own strength and love of power,

and knew how to honour it: they honoured some-thing in themselves when they honoured the saint. In addition to this, the contemplation of the saint suggested to them a suspicion: such an enormity of self-negation and anti-naturalness will not have been coveted for nothing. . . . In a word, the mighty ones of the world learned to have a new fear before him, they divined a new power, a strange, still unconquered enemy:—it was the "Will to Power" which obliged them to halt before the saint. They had to question him. (56)

Nietzsche's insight is confirmed by Cioran, who on the first page of *Tears and Saints* spells out the reason for his interest in saints in the form of a question his book promises to explore: "How does a man renounce him-self and take the road to sainthood?" In the saints' ability to renounce the world, Cioran detects their "will to power": saintliness, he writes, is "imperialistic," it "interests me for the delirium of self-aggrandizement hidden beneath its meekness, its will to power masked by goodness." Clearly fascinated by this will to power in a political world torn by extreme claims, from fascism to communism, Cioran nonetheless regards it with an awe tinged by ironic skepticism. He looks upon saints as partial alter egos, devout existentialists who "live *in* flames" while "wise men live *next* to them." His relation-ship to them as it develops in the book is one of both love and hatred. "I love saints for their passionate na-iveté," he writes at one point. His love for the saints has a shade of decadent aestheticism in it: "we no longer be-lieve in them. We only admire their illusions." However, such dandified love is counterbalanced by a vigorous and virulent hatred. He confesses many times that he hates the saints for the habit of hopeless suffering that they bequeathed to us, since suffering "can't be anything but futile and satanic." How could one not hate saints, angels, and God? . . . Heaven irritates me, its Christian disguise drives me to despair."

Tears and Saints is a meditation on saintliness, but not saintliness of the usual type. That is, not the martyrs and heroes of traditional hagiography, worshiped for their virtues, but rather the mystics famous for their high degree of spirituality, their intimate personal knowledge of God, who brought about a new "eruption of the absolute into history." The title, *Tears and Saints*, refers to what is known in the tradition of the Roman Catholic Church as the "gift of tears." The *Dictionnaire de la spiritualité* describes "the gift of tears" as "a complex phenomenon consisting of certain spiritual feelings and their concrete manifestation." It cites three categories of holy tears: penitential tears (purifying tears of fear and regret), tears of love (or grace), and tears of compassion wept for the Passion of Christ. Starting with Francis of Assisi in the early thirteenth century, the latter kind became predominant.

The tears of pity for the suffering Christ, to which Cioran alludes repeatedly in his text, are a characteristic feature of Western European mysticism. Mysticism is "a movement towards an object outside the limits of empirical experience." It is also a "direct and passive experience of God's presence" (*Dictionnaire de la spiritualité*). This "movement" is an escape—through prayer, meditation and contemplation—from the here and now. It aims at reunion with God, and it is centered on the mystery of the Incarnation and Redemption because the humanity of Christ is perceived as mediation between man and God. Through sympathetic identification with the suffering Christ, one is redeemed from one's "fallen" state and reunited with God, thereby partaking of his divinity. Tears were perceived as a sign of grace, the external manifestation of God's presence in the human heart. Many descriptions of this gift insist on its ineffable sweetness. Cioran puts a twist on mystical discourse from the very beginning, since for him tears are not sweet but bitter: "As I searched for the origin of tears, I thought of the saints. Could they be the source of tears' bitter light?"

The saints in Cioran's title belong to a new class of saints, mostly lay and mostly female, called "mystics," "spirituels," "contemplatifs," or "alumbrados." Their approach to the Christian faith is antitheological and antiinstitutional, based solely on intuition and sentiment. Many of the names in this book, Meister Eckhart, Catherine of Siena, Teresa of Avila, St. John of the Cross, have left classic works of Western European mystical literature, but there are many more minor and unusual figures as well. In *Tears and Saints*, Cioran subsumes mystics under the name of saints. Since for him mystics are apolitical, passive contemplators of divinity, he prefers to call them saints. Saints, he writes, are politicians—though "failed" ones, because they deny appearances: pragmatic men and women of action, whose acts of charity express their love of humankind. Indeed, many of the European mystics were active reformers, serious players in the game of European politics (Catherine of Siena, for example, played a political role in bringing the pope back to Rome from Avignon). And all of them—many belonging to the mendicant orders—were dedicated to charity work in the world outside the monastery walls, assiduously tending the poor and the ill.

European mysticism is a religious movement with political overtones. It is marked by a strong spirit of reform, which developed in the margins of—and often at odds with—the official institution of the Catholic Church, which these saintly persons perceived as degraded and corrupt, no longer capable of caring fully for the spiritual needs of the population. Historically, it covers several centuries and several Western European countries, from its inception (with Bernard of Clairvaux in the twelfth century), to its vigorous expansion at the end of the thirteenth century in Germany and Holland and then into Italy, through its apogee in sixteenth-century Spain, and its final afterglow in seventeenth-century France just before the Age of Reason. Although it spans many centuries, European mysticism is, as Michel de Certeau observes in *The Mystic Fable*, a "borderline" phenomenon, occurring on the threshold of modernity, at a time when unified Christian Europe is disintegrating, strong secular states are formed, and the bases of new sciences and arts are set. Thus "the ambition of a Christian radicalism [is] traced on a background of decadence or 'corruption,' within a universe that is falling apart and must be repaired" (Certeau, 14). Faced with the breakdown of the Christian faith and "the humiliation of the Christian tradition," the mystics rise to fight for the restoration of true faith. For example, Teresa of Avila and St. John of the Cross were reformers of their orders. They thus formed a "Christian radicalism," verging on heresy, "waver[ing] between ecstasy and revolt" (Certeau, 24).

Cioran explicitly focuses on the political element in the saints' lives, but in his view their charitable deeds represent the least interesting aspect of their lives. What fascinates him are their tears, their thirst for pain and their capacity to endure it: in short, the pathology or, as he puts it, the "voluptuousness of suffering," for "suffering is man's only biography." Behind this suffering, and their uncanny ability to renounce everything through ascetic practices, Cioran detects the saints' fanatical will to power.

Saints' writings are often titled "Dialogues" because they are presented in the form of a dialogue with God, "conversar con Dios" as Teresa of Avila called it. In his analysis of mystical discourse, Certeau observes that a main feature of the saints' writings is the initial assertion of will, the opening "volo," "I want," which is both ecstatic, signifying a decision to escape, and ascetic, signifying a decision to lose (Certeau, 229). This act of willing, "vouloir," is at the same time an act of power, "pouvoir," writes Certeau. He cites one of the classics of mysticism, Meister Eckhart, who said: "With the will I can do everything," and "what I want to have, I have" (Certeau, 170). But what do the saints want to possess and control? "Their space to conquer is the sky, their weapon suffering," says Cioran. The saints' "will to power" has no object in particular. They want to own infinity ("the sky") and God: i.e., they want an absence, for, as Baudelaire once remarked, "God is the only being who, in order to rule, does not even need to exist." Thus inner space is the region in which the will reigns supreme, enjoying an autonomy that does not depend on object or circumstance (Certeau, 235–36), and the heart or the soul is the stage on which the mystical drama is enacted as, for example, in Teresa of Avila's *Las moradas*.

It is this fanatical but also gratuitous will to power, to know and to love, or to know through love— directed at all and at the same time at nothing, i.e., God—that engrosses Cioran's attention in *Tears and Saints*. But whereas for the saints God is meaningful nothingness, for Cioran, as for Nietzsche, "God is dead," and nothingness is devoid of meaning. Thus the book is a critique of this will to power which reaps nothing but empty and cruel suffering. It both reveals and rejects the political roots of sainthood, and finally inscribes itself in the psychological or aesthetic sphere since saints are, after all, "failed politicians," who stubbornly deny the world of appearances.

Nonetheless, to speak of the saints' "will to power" does uncover a political aspect of their existential religious experience, and brings the question of politics in this book sharply into focus. That is why the historical context of the production and publication of *Tears and Saints* is important. The book appeared soon after Cioran's departure for Paris in 1937, the year in which he also published his most radical and overtly political book, *Romania's Transfiguration*. The two contemporaneous books form an interesting pair: one, a metacritical discourse on mysticism, the other a political tract couched in the rhetoric of mysticism. *Tears and*

Saints was published at Cioran's own expense after his publisher, halfway into the printing process, became aware of the shocking nature of the text and refused to bring it out. Cioran has told me how he had to leave the press with the galley proofs in a bag, carrying them through Bucharest in search of another publisher.

When it did appear, *Tears and Saints* caused a scandal. Written in short, aphoristic fragments, strongly reminiscent of Nietzsche both in form and in content, it is a discontinuous and iconoclastic philosophical discourse on mysticism. The aura of decadence that goes with the book's anti-Christian, blasphemous tone was unheard of in Romania. But as Huysmans says of his decadent hero, Des Esseintes, in *A Rebours,* one must be a Catholic first in order to desecrate Catholicism. There is a strong Christian current stirring under the anti-Christian surface of Cioran's prose. One must remember that Cioran was the son of an Orthodox priest, and therefore very familiar with the doctrines of the Christian faith. His younger brother in Romania recalls long nights spent around bottles of wine, during which Cioran argued intricate theological questions with his father and theologians from the seminary in Sibiu. According to his brother, Cioran's chief obsessions at the time were theology and music, a fact confirmed by Cioran's text—as always an exorcism of his obsessions—in which fine aphorisms on music intertwine with his musings on tears and saints.

As a discourse on spirituality, asceticism, and suffering for the love of Christ, *Tears and Saints* inscribes itself strongly in the historical, philosophical, and political discourses circulating in the Romania of the 1920s and

1930s. "Spirituality" was so much the talk of Romanian interwar culture that a leading journal, *Criterion*, devoted a long article to it in its "Dictionary" column, which tried to define the "principal ideas" of the period and establish their "circulation value." In particular, the article identified "the problem of a 'new spirituality' with that of the 'new generation'" to which Cioran belonged.

As Nietzsche said, those interested in the figure of the saint are never ordinary but always the "mightiest men." Cioran's "young generation" of intellectuals was an elite group of strong-minded people, a generation driven by a sense of mission, namely, the regeneration of Romania. They saw themselves as representatives of a "new revolutionary spirituality" which, according to the *Criterion* article, both overlaps and at the same time rejects other types of spirituality present in contemporary Romanian culture: the traditional, orthodox spirituality of the charismatic philosophy professor and mentor of the new generation, Nae Ionescu, or the more "cultural" and humanistic type of other young intellectuals such as Petru Comarnescu or Constantin Noica. Mircea Vulcanescu, the author of the *Criterion* article and himself a member of this generation, estimated that large numbers of young writers, "led by Mircea Eliade," embraced the new "agonic spirituality" whose main characteristics were "lucidity, negation, and a tragic doubt that wants itself invalidated by the revelation of a new type of man, yet to be born."

This generation of intellectuals had political ties with the Legion of the Archangel Michael, later known as the Iron Guard, "a populist movement with strong mystical characteristics," bent on bringing about "moral and spiritual change, ethnic 'regeneration' by returning to Orthodox Christian values, and 'salvation' through asceticism and sacrifice" (Volovici, 62). Cioran's generation of young intellectuals was sympathetic to the Legionary movement because they believed it to be the only political means capable of triggering a "Christian revolution" that would lead to the creation of a Christian state. Against a background of extreme political corruption and economic deterioration, moved by a strong sense of an ending, caught between nostalgia for Paradise Lost and impatience for a New Jerusalem, these young, modern-day "saints" were animated by a desire to reform which, unfortunately, found its political counterpart in the fascistic Iron Guard.

It is fairly easy to trace the similarities between the historical conditions that gave rise to Western European mysticism and the mystical mania that swept Romania in the 1930s. *Mutatis mutandis,* both periods were characterized by an identity crisis and the responsibility to reform politically and spiritually. As Certeau puts it, there is in history a certain tendency towards *coincidence* between a "Machiavellian moment" and "the invasion of the mystics" (Certeau, 153). Thus "the task of producing a Republic or a State by political reason that would take the place of a defunct, illegible, divine order, in a way [was] paralleled by the task of founding places in which to hear the spoken Word that had become inaudible within corrupt institutions" (Certeau, 154). In fact, one could argue, as Certeau does, that European mysticism did not die in the seventeenth century but simply receded: "this phantom of a passage, repressed during periods secure in their knowledge, reappears in the gaps within scientific certainty, as if ever returning to its birthplace" (Certeau, 77–78). "Secure" and "certainty" are the key words here. Europe in the first half of the twentieth century was wrenched by momentous upheavals. In the tormented European political and intellectual context, Romania, probably more than any other country in Europe, given its political and economic coordinates, dramatically lacked certainty about itself and thus became fertile ground for a rebirth of mysticism in political garb.

It is in this intellectual and political context that *Tears and Saints* must be read, both as an expression of, and a reaction to, the spirit of the times. Its mystical frenzy, tempered by an irony verging on blasphemy, makes it stand apart, as it certainly did in its reviled and scandalous reception in Romania.

A closer look at Cioran's other 1937 book, *Romania's Transfiguration*, helps us to appreciate the distinct note struck by *Tears and Saints* in its historical context. Whereas the latter is a critique of mystical discourse, *Romania's Transfiguration* borrows the rhetoric of mystical discourse and applies it to the realm of politics. The book is a political utopia dreaming of a "transfigured" or redeemed Romania, of a Romania capable of breaking its "subhistoric" destiny, and from a "secondhand country" becoming a "great culture." In *Tears and Saints*, Cioran defines saintliness as the "overcoming of our condition as fallen creatures." In mysticism, redemption and the saints' will to possess God are in fact one and the same thing. That is why the formula for redemption need not remain confined to the spiritual domain and can easily be translated into political terms: the mystic's spiritual union with God becomes a (small) nation's fulfillment of a greater destiny: "Our entire political and spiritual mission must concentrate on the determination to *will* a transfiguration, on the desperate and dramatic experience of transforming our whole way of life" (*Romania's Transfiguration*, 47).

In *Romania's Transfiguration*, Cioran gives us his solution to Romania's identity crisis: Romania will overcome its "fallen" historical condition as a "little culture" only when it is driven by a fanaticism equal to that of the saints. Here the mystical "will" is not object-less, it has a specific political content, and its stage is not the heart or the soul but history itself:

> *Romania is a prophetless country.* . . . This sobering thought should prompt us to be different, to burn with a blind fanaticism, to be illuminated by a new vision. . . . and the thought of another Romania should be our only thought. To persist in the same historical sequence is the equivalent of slow suicide. . . . We shall have to renounce our lucidity which reveals to us so many impossibilities, and, in a state of blindness, conquer the light. . . . (*Romania's Transfiguration*, 49; emphasis added)

Couched in the mystical language of ecstatic visions, the will to bring about spiritual reform is coupled here with the will to achieve cultural greatness. To bring about this end, all means are justified in the eyes of the young Cioran, who sounds like a new Machiavelli, thus confirming Certeau's insight that mysticism and Machiavellianism often coincide:

> All means are legitimate when a people opens a road for itself in the world. Terror, crime, bestiality and perfidy are base and immoral only in decadence, when they defend a vacuum of content; if, on the other hand, they help in the ascension of a people, they are virtues. All triumphs are moral. . . . (*Romania's Transfiguration*, 41)

Cioran's Machiavelli knows his Nietzsche. The passage quoted echoes *Beyond Good and Evil*, where, comparing decadent to nondecadent historical periods, Nietzsche writes:

> Certain strong and dangerous instincts, such as the love of enterprise, foolhardiness, revengefulness, astuteness, rapacity, and love of power, which up till then had not only to be honoured from the point of view of general utility—under other names, of course, than those given—but had to be fostered and cultivated (because they were perpetually required in the common danger against the common enemies), are now felt in their dangerousness to be doubly strong—when the outlets for them are lacking—and are gradually branded as immoral and given over to calumny. (*Beyond Good and Evil*, 124)

We are thus faced with an interesting intellectual situation: two books by the same author published in the same year, both suffused with mysticism, the one ra-

bidly political, the other a critical analysis of the
political roots of mystical discourse. One might be
tempted to say that while *Tears and Saints* is a philosophical dissertation on the mystical phenomenon,
scrutinizing its political implications, *Romania's Transfiguration,* its unfortunate political counterpart, is a
rather crude practical application of mystical principles,
very much in step with other politico-religious right-
wing or left-wing discourses of the period. But Cioran's
ambiguous attitude towards mysticism in *Tears and Saints*
shows that *Romania's Transfiguration* is in his mind, at the
very moment he is writing the latter, a political utopia,
i.e., a "delirium of self-aggrandizement." Its mystical
overtones strongly contribute to its utopian, delirious
character, which contradicts Cioran's existential philosophy of skepticism and despair. In *Tears and Saints,*
Cioran's love-hate relationship with the mystic saints
problematizes the simple and fanatical solution to Romania's problems he offers in *Romania's Transfiguration.*
Thus *Tears and Saints* is in some ways Cioran's philosophical struggle with himself, a text full of contradictions
and ambiguities; appearing at the same time as *Romania's
Transfiguration,* and out of the same preoccupations, it reveals the shortcomings of his other, crudely naive
political text, and thereby undermines it.

Many of the themes in *Tears and Saints* are ones to which
Cioran will return again and again in his later, mature
writings: music, spirituality, suffering, death, solitude,
doubt, despair, decadence, God, and nothingness. As a
discourse on mysticism, *Tears and Saints* is neither mystical discourse nor objective, impersonal philosophical

discourse. Generically, it resembles Nietzsche's hybrid philosophical commentary. The free and easy colloquial and lyrical style, studded with striking metaphors, and the personal, intimate, alternately tongue-in-cheek and vehement tones mask the extent of the text's erudition, its "bookishness," as well as the accuracy and seriousness of its commentary on the mystical phenomenon. The ambiguous, often paradoxical nature of *Tears and Saints* originates in its fundamental oscillation between two opposite drives, the intense longing to believe with passion and abandon—an attitude also informing *Romania's Transfiguration*—and the passion of disbelief, i.e., of despair.

The book's central figure is Cioran's "failed mystic," "the one who cannot cast off all temporal ties." Thus he writes that "the secret of successful mysticism is the defeat of time and individuation," but also "I can't help hearing a death knell ringing in eternity: therein lies my quarrel with mysticism"—anticipating Derrida's *Glas* by almost half a century. The "failed mystic" is a strikingly grotesque character: "the passion of the absolute in the soul of a skeptic is like an angel grafted on a leper." He belongs to the same family of existential outcasts, forever wandering in the no-man's-land stretching between history and eternity, as Unamuno's martyr, Manuel Bueno, Dostoevsky's Ivan Karamazov, or Genet's "criminal saint."

There is no redemption for Cioran's failed mystic. While the successful mystics praise as the apogee of ecstasy the moment in which they feel alone with God, what St. John of the Cross calls "soledad en Dios," Cioran complains that he cannot feel "at home in

God," that he is a perpetual "exile in Him." For the "successful" mystic, God is *the* object of desire, the target of his will to power, but for Cioran, no matter how hard he strives to love and to believe in a mystical way, his fervor is always undermined by doubt and despair. He is haunted by Nietzsche's "God is dead" (or as Cioran more humorously puts it, God is "a Universal absentee"). He unmasks the saints' unforgivable naiveté: they "have never asked themselves the question 'what begins *after* God?' and for that I cannot forgive them." The despair of this failed mystic—"My God without you I'm mad, and with you I shall go mad!"—as well as his existential doubts—"my doubts cannot take me farther than the shadow of His heart"—are mixed in with a touch of bravado, a romantic, Luciferian pose. Our role, he says, is to amuse a lonely God, we are "poor clowns of the absolute." But he refused to play his part in God's entertainment piece, in a daring act of "rejection of God sprung from agonic frenzy": "I, with my solitude, stand up to God."

Centered on the figure of the failed mystic, Cioran's discourse on mysticism is a sort of self-consciously blasphemous parody of mystical discourse. The voice of the faithless mystic introduces a new perspective, that of despair, and thus gives a new accent to the mystical experience, deliberately and perversely distorting its meanings. For example, "paradise from the view point of despair" becomes "a graveyard of happiness." In the mystical experience, meditation and prayer are important steps towards God, but for Cioran they are exactly the opposite: "one must think of God day and night in order to wear him out, to turn him into a cliché." For the mystics, life in God is the only true life; for Cioran, it is "the death of being."

The most frequent target of his attack, however, is a key aspect of mysticism: suffering, the imitation of the Man-God's agonistic passion as the only means to reach the divine. The mystic's suffering has as its goal redemption, i.e., to achieve perfection in divinity. Cioran, however, approaches suffering from an aesthetic rather than ethical point of view since it is the "voluptuousness of suffering," not its virtues, that fascinates him. He sees suffering as essential to the tragic human condition—"suffering is man's only biography"—and as aimless, since it does not hold out the promise of redemption inherent in Christian notions of suffering, carried to extremes by mysticism. Suffering, behind which Cioran detected the will to power, is ineffectual, it achieves nothing except more senseless and cruel suffering. There is no room for redemption in a world in which, "since the creation of consciousness, God has appeared in his true light as one more nothingness." The despair of the failed mystic, bereft of his greatest hope, and overcome by what Unamuno called "el sentimiento tragico de la vida," takes the form of Nietzschean attacks on Christianity. In these attacks, Cioran's voice is by turns virulent and ironic: "I don't know any bigger sin than that of Jesus"; "the ultimate cruelty was that of Jesus: leaving an inheritance of bloodstains on the cross"; Jesus, "the bloodthirsty and cruel" Christ, was "lucky to have died young. Had he lived to be sixty, he would have given us his memoirs instead of the cross." In a passage that recalls past catastrophes caused by excesses in the history of Christianity, and also anticipates the excesses that will be soon carried out in his own country, Cioran, fascinated with sacred violence and suffering, writes, decades before Georges Bataille's *Larmes d'Eros* or René Girard's *Violence and the Sacred*, that "Christianity delights in the sight of bloodstains, its martyrs have transformed the world into a bloodbath. In this religion of blazing twilights, evil defeats the sublime."

If the mystical formula ultimately fails for Cioran in the spiritual domain, it follows that its political counterpart is also doomed to fail. Could this man of so many doubts and shadows have been doing anything else but raving in a fit of impotent rage or a "delirium of self-aggrandizement" when he wrote *Romania's Transfiguration?* Could he, like Unamuno's failed saint, Manuel Bueno, have been preaching that in which he himself cannot believe? If *Romania's Transfiguration* tried to offer a solution to Romania's existential and political problems, its contemporary counterpart, *Tears and Saints*, reveals the other side of the coin, namely, that there are no solutions where there is only honest, despairing doubt. Thus through *Tears and Saints* we gain a perspective on Cioran's complex and divided mind exactly at the time he was writing his most outrageous political tract:

> the soul of those haunted by God is like a depraved spring, littered with half-withered flowers and rotten buds, swept by foul odors. It is the soul of blackmailing saints . . . and of anti-Christian Christians such as Nietzsche. I regret that I'm not Judas to betray God and know remorse.

In the Romania of the 1930s, Cioran's young soul was haunted by two absolutes, neither of which he could believe in. Given this situation, his next step seems inevitable: if not suicide, then self-exile. In 1937, a few months before the publication of *Tears and Saints*, he left Bucharest and never returned. When we next hear of him, in Paris in 1949, the year of his first French book, *Précis de décomposition*, he has cast off both his Romanian language and identity, and yielded to a long-cherished obsession: to be a man from nowhere.

Acknowledgments
I thank E. M. Cioran for allowing me to translate yet another one of his books, and Mme Simone Boué for many long and lovely Parisian evenings when I imbibed the Cioranian spirit at leisure. For dedicated and inspired editing, I thank my husband, Kenneth R. Johnston.

This translation was made possible by grants from the National Endowment for the Arts and from Indiana University (Office of Research and Graduate Development, Russian and Eastern Institute, and West European Studies).

Note on the Text
This translation aims at capturing the spirit of Cioran's original Romanian, not a literal, word-for-word accuracy. Principally, this has meant a trimming of Cioran's youthful prose, mainly those passages that sound florid or redundant in English. However, this English translation, unlike an earlier French version which was

drastically cut by the author, restores Cioran's text to its original length.

Ilinca Zarifopol-Johnston

Works Cited

Baudelaire, Charles. *Oeuvres Complètes.* Paris: Gallimard, 1975.

Cioran, E. M. *Schimbarea la Fata a Romaniei* (Romania's Trans-figuration). Bucharest: Vremea, 1937.

De Certeau, Michel. *The Mystic Fable,* trans. Michael B. Smith. Chicago: University of Chicago Press, 1992.

Nietzsche, Friedrich. *Beyond Good and Evil,* trans. Helen Zimern. New York: Russell and Russell, 1964.

Volovici, Leon. *Nationalist Ideology and Anti-Semitism: The Case of Romanian Intellectuals in the 1930s.* Oxford: Pergamon Press, 1991.

Vulcánescu, Mircea, "Spiritualitate." *Criterion* (Bucharest): 1 November 1934.

Dictionnaire de la spiritualité ascétique et mystique. Paris: Beauchesne, 1976.

TEARS AND SAINTS

As I searched for the origin of tears, I thought of the saints. Could they be the source of tears' bitter light? Who can tell? To be sure, tears are their *trace.* Tears did not enter this world through the saints; but without them we would have never known that we cry because we long for a lost paradise. Show me a single tear swallowed up by the earth! No, by paths unknown to us, they all go upwards. Pain comes before tears. But the saints rehabilitated them.

Saints cannot be *known.* Only when we awaken the tears sleeping in our depths and know *through* them, do we come to understand how someone could renounce being a man.

Sainthood in itself is not interesting, only the lives of the saints are. How does a man renounce himself and take the road to sainthood? But then how does one become a hagiographer? By following in their traces, by wetting the soles of one's feet in their tears!

Djelal-eddin-Rumi: "The voice of the violin is the sound of the opening gate of paradise."

To what then can one compare the sigh of an angel?

What shall we tell the blind woman in Rilke's poem who lamented that "I can no longer live with the sky upon me"? Would it comfort her if we told her we can no longer live with the earth underneath our feet?

Many saints—but especially saintly women—confessed a desire to rest their head on the heart of Jesus. They all had their wish fulfilled. Now I understand why Our Redeemer's heart has not ceased to beat for two thousand years. My Lord! You fed your heart on the blood of the saints, and you bathed it in the sweat of their brows!

How can we not love Saint Teresa who, on the day Jesus revealed himself to her as her betrothed, ran out into the courtyard of the nunnery and began to dance in a frenzy, beating a drum, inviting the sisters to join in her ecstatic joy?

When she was six years old, she read the lives of the saints and her heart responded with shouts of "Eternity, eternity!" It was then that she decided to convert the Arabs, at the risk of her life. She did not fulfill her wish; her passion, however, grew. The fire in her soul has not died even today, since we still live in its heat.

To win the guilty kiss of a saint, I'd welcome the plague as a blessing.

✦

Shall I ever be so pure that only saints' tears could be my mirror?

✦

Strange, that there can be several saints living at the same time. I try to imagine a meeting of saints, but neither my imagination nor my enthusiasm help me much. The fifty-two-year-old Saint Teresa, famous and much admired, meeting a twenty-five-year-old Saint John of the Cross, anonymous yet full of passion, in Medina del Campo! Spanish mysticism: a divine moment in the history of humanity.

Saints' dialogues? A Shakespeare with the heart of a virgin could write them, or a Dostoevsky exiled in a heavenly Siberia. I shall prowl after saints all my life.

Perhaps no one built more roads to God out of music and dance than Djelal-eddin-Rumi, a saint long since canonized by his admirers. His meeting with Chems-eddin, anonymous pilgrim and uneducated wise man, is full of strange charm. After they met, they locked themselves up for three months in Djelal-eddin's house in Konia, and did not leave it for one moment all that time. A sort of instinctive certainty makes me think that everything was said there.

In those times, people cultivated their secrets. You could speak to God at any time, and he would bury your sighs in his nothingness. Now we are inconsolable because we have no one to speak to. We have been reduced to confessing our loneliness to mortals. This world must

5

once have lived *in* God. History divides itself in two: a former time when people felt pulled towards the vibrant nothingness of divinity and now, when the nothingness of the world is empty of the divine spirit.

Music makes me too bold in front of God. This is what distances me from the Oriental mystics.

Only tears will be weighed at the Last Judgment.

The heart of Jesus was the Christians' pillow. I understand those mystics who longed to lay their heads on it! But my doubts take me no farther than the shadow of his heart.

No one truly understands sainthood if he does not feel that the heart is its world. *The heart as universe*—this is the deepest meaning of sainthood. *Everything happens in the heart:* that's mysticism and saintliness. But this doesn't mean people's hearts, only saints' hearts.

Sainthood is transfigured physiology, maybe even divine physiology. Every bodily *function* becomes a movement towards the sky. Blood is one of its constant obsessions. Saintliness is a triumph over blood.

The purified blood of Jesus is the saints' bath and their drink. Thus Catherine of Siena's last words: "Oh blood!" She was referring to the merits of Our Savior's blood.

The difference between mystics and saints is that the former stop at an inner vision, while the latter put it into practice. Saintliness suffers the consequences of mysticism, especially on the ethical side. A saint is a mystic, a mystic may not be a saint. Charity is not a necessary attribute of mysticism; but we cannot conceive of saintliness without it. Ethics plus mysticism gives birth to the intriguing phenomenon of sainthood. The mystics cultivate a heavenly sensuality, a voluptuousness born of their intercourse with the sky; only saints take on their shoulders the load of others, the suffering of unknown people; only they act. Compared to the pure mystic, the saint is a politician. Next to the mystic, the saint is the most active of men. Yet their troubled lives are not *biographies* because they are one-dimensional, variations on a single theme: absolute passion.

"The mystic is a man who tells you about your mystery while you remain silent." (I don't remember the great Oriental who offered this definition.)

✧

Eyes don't see. Catherine of Emmerich was right to say that she saw only *through the heart*. Such is the sight of saints. How could they not see more than us, who see only through our senses? The eye has a limited field; it always sees from the outside. But with the world in your heart, introspection is the only mode of knowing. The heart's visual space = God + the world + nothingness. That is, everything.

The eye can *magnify*; in the heart everything is *magnificent*. I understand Mechthild of Magdeburg when she laments that neither the beauty of the world nor the saints can comfort her, nothing but Jesus and his heart. Neither mystics nor saints need eyes; they don't look at the world. Their heart is their eye.

✧

Living with saints, as with music or books, is unmanning. One's instincts begin to serve another world. To the extent that we resist saintliness, we prove the health of our instincts.

✧

The empire of the sky occupies territory emptied of vitality. Heavenly imperialism aims at biological neutrality.

How does music suck our blood? Man cannot live without support in *space*. But music annihilates space completely. The only art capable of bringing comfort, yet it opens up more wounds than all the others!

Music is the sound track of *askesis*. Could one make love after Bach? Not even after Handel, whose unearthliness does not have a heavenly perfume. Music is a tomb of delights, beatitude which buries us.

Saintliness also draws blood. We lose it in direct proportion to our longing for heaven. The roads to heaven have been worn smooth by all the erring instincts. Indeed, heaven was born of these errors.

✧

Djelal-eddin-Rumi speaks of the five senses of the heart. In them lies the gnosis of mysticism. Ecstasy, as a supreme expression of mystical knowledge, is all senses melted into one flame.

✧

My Lord, without you I'm mad, and with you I shall go mad!

✧

Love for mankind renders saints uninteresting. Their virtue has no biographical interest. When we talk of love, only God can make us ward off banality.

Were it not for all that love in the saints' lives, they alone would deserve our love. Their absolute love makes them incomplete. Saints, who never erred out of pain and only knew love, are so colorless that not even a heavenly ray can brighten them.

Love is the saints' commonplace. Were it not for their tears and sighs, we would find little interest in their excess of love.

✧

Those who are in love with saintly women cannot help being jealous of Jesus. Why should one love someone else's lover? Would there be a kiss left for us after all those ecstasies and embraces? Their smile is unpromising, for Jesus comes first in their hearts.

✧

Without the *voluptuousness of suffering*, saintliness would not interest us any more than a medieval political intrigue in some little provincial town. Suffering is man's only biography; its *voluptuousness*, the saint's.

To be a saint, never miss a single opportunity among the infinite varieties of agony.

Rose of Lima, born in South America apparently to redeem Pizarro's crimes, is a model for all those with a vocation for suffering. Young and beautiful, she could not think of an excuse to resist her mother's wish to bring her out in society. But she finally found a compromise. Under the crown of flowers on her head she pinned a needle that pricked her forehead incessantly. Thus she satisfied her desire to be alone in society. One conquers the temptation of the world through pain. Pascal's belt belongs to this tradition of suffering.

For whom did Rose of Lima put a needle in her

crown? The heavenly lover made a new victim. Jesus was the Don Juan of agony.

Saintliness is the negation of life through heavenly hysteria. How does one negate life? Through uninterrupted lucidity. Hence the saints' almost total suppression of sleep. Rose of Lima never slept more than two hours a night, and when she felt that sleep was overpowering her, she would hang herself on a cross in her room, or force herself to stand by tying her hair to a nail.

Saintliness is a special kind of madness. While the madness of mortals exhausts itself in useless and fantastic actions, holy madness is a conscious effort towards winning everything.

Competing with Jesus, the saints' excesses repeat Golgotha, adding to it the refinements of torture gleaned from subsequent Christian centuries. Christ's crown of thorns, imitated by the saints, caused more suffering in the world than I don't know how many incurable diseases. Jesus was, after all, the saints' incurable disease. Rose of Lima also used to wear under her veil a crown of nails that wounded her at every movement. They say that once her father touched her head accidentally and streams of blood flowed from her wounds. Often she was seen bearing a huge cross, miming with amazing intensity the Golgotha of her heavenly lover.

Jesus is responsible for so much suffering. His conscience must weigh on him very heavily, since he no longer gives any signs of life. To tell the truth, he does not stand comparison with his followers. In them, his heavenly passion has become a virus. Instead of roses, they gave us thorns. I don't know any bigger sin than that of Jesus.

Prolonged interest in saintliness is an illness which requires a few years' convalescence. Then, you are seized by a desire to pick up your sadness and roam under another sky, to grow strong elsewhere. The need for *space* is a counter-reaction to the infinity of saintliness. You feel like lying in the grass and looking up at the sky, free from the prejudice of its heights.

Paganism is the deepening of appearances, while saintliness is the sickness of depths.

"I cannot differentiate between tears and music" (Nietzsche). Whoever is not immediately struck by the profundity of this statement has not lived for a minute in the intimacy of music. I know no other music than that of tears. Born out of the loss of paradise, music gives birth to the *symbols* of this loss: tears.

Catherine of Siena lived only on communion bread. Easy to do when you have heaven to back you up! Ecstasy destroys the fruit of the earth. She drank the sky in the Eucharist. For the faithful, communion, that tiny particle of heaven, is infinitely more nutritious than earthly food. Why do the heights require the suppression of appetite? Why do poets, musicians, mystics, and saints use *askesis* in various ways? Voluntary hunger is a road to heaven; hunger from poverty, a crime of the earth.

Saintliness would be a most extraordinary phenomenon, even more than divinity, if it had any practical value. The passionate desire of saints to take over the sins and sufferings of mortals is well known. Many outbursts of infinite pity could be cited to confirm this. But in spite of all that, do the bitterness and sufferings of others diminish at all? Except for their capacity to comfort, the saints' effort is useless, and the practical achievements of their love are nothing but a monumental illusion. One cannot suffer for another. How much can your increased suffering relieve the suffering of your neighbor? Were the saints to understand this simple matter, they would probably become politicians; that is, they would no longer be ashamed of appearances. Only appearances can be changed. But saints are politicians afraid of appearances. Thus they deprive themselves of matter and space for their exercise in reform. One cannot love both suffering and appearances at once. In this respect, saintliness is not equivocal. A vocation for appearances ties most of us to life. It frees us from saintliness.

"None of my sufferings has been equal to that of not having suffered enough" (Margaret-Mary Alacoque). A classic expression of the avidity for pain.

No mental state is less creative than mild sadness, the very negation of inspiration. Everything depends on the *level* of sadness, on the frequency of its vibrations. At a certain level it is poetical, at another musical, and finally religious. Thus there are different kinds of sadness: of poets, of musicians, of saints. The sadness of poets or musicians leaves their heart, goes around the world, and returns like an echo. The sadness of saints also leaves the heart but it stops in God, thus fulfilling every saint's secret wish, to become his prisoner.

Until about the eighteenth century, there was a wealth of treatises on human perfection. Almost everyone who stopped halfway on the road to saintliness wrote such a book as a consolation, so that for centuries perfection was the obsession of all failed saints. Those who succeeded no longer cared about it, since they *possessed* it.

Later centuries shifted their attitude to one of total disengagement, looking on perfection with great suspicion and unmistakable spite. For modern man, there's no greater shame than perfection. Having overcome his longing for paradise, he managed to rid himself of perfection at the same time. During Christian times, people were proud of their saints. We only "appreciate" them. If we think we love them, it's only our weakness which brings them closer for a moment.

What secret voice whispers to me that if I could have all the saints on one side, their hearts dancing like flames between heaven and earth, and Nero on the other, frozen in a state half-imbecilic, half-melancholic, I would open my heart to the latter? Nero's boredom was greater than the Christians' thirst for heaven. Even the great fire of Rome seemed to him banal. Boredom gives birth to madness—or is it vice versa? Nero was a melancholy man. Otherwise why would he have loved music? The destiny of this man, bored by the whole world, is moving. We have forgotten his one redeeming feature, his *lyre.*

When you are born with a strong presentiment of death, life advances toward birth in reverse. It recovers all of the stages of life in a sort of upside-down evolution: you die, then you live, suffer, and finally are born. Or is it another life that is born on the ruins of death? One feels the need to love, suffer, and be born again only after having known death in *oneself.* The only life is the one after death. That's why transfigurations are so rare.

Saints live *in* flames; wise men, next to them.

Beethoven overcomes too often the temptation of sadness. Such self-restraint alienates him from me. By comparison, Chopin and Schumann are connoisseurs of voluptuous sadness. Beethoven seems proud of the triumphs of will over sadness. He was more a connoisseur of despair, that wounded pride of the will battling with the world.

We would have been better off without saints. Then each of us would have minded our own business and we would have rejoiced in our imperfection. Their presence among us brings about useless inferiority complexes, envy, spite. The world of the saints is a heavenly poison that grows ever more virulent as our loneliness increases. They have corrupted us by providing a model that shows suffering attaining its goal. We are used to suffering aimlessly, lost in the uselessness of pain; we are used to mirroring ourselves in our own blood. However, we should not regret it too much, for suffering does not necessarily lead to heaven.

Despair, more than any other feeling, establishes a correspondence between our being and the environment. In fact, despair requires a corresponding environment to such an extent that, if need be, it creates it. It invokes beauty only to pour the void into it. The emptiness of the soul is so vast, its cruel advance so inexorable, that any resistance to it is impossible. What would be left of paradise if it were seen from the viewpoint of despair? A graveyard of happiness.

Landscapes that do not trigger musical themes cannot become memories. Whoever has not roamed through parks in a state of elation and melancholy can never understand Mozart's grace. Solemn evenings without Brahms, or monumental nature without Beethoven? Music has a cosmic character. The passion for music has no basis without love of nature.

"A rain of roses will fall at my death" (Thérèse of Lisieux).
"Rose, you exude the perfume of a naked saint's body" (R. M. Rilke).

Funereal echoes in Mozart's grace: whoever has not discovered them does not know that grace is a triumph over sadness, and that there is only melancholy grace. A Mozart andante does not always invite us to happiness.

His concerto in A Major for piano and orchestra, for example. Mozart may have had an A Major soul, but with all the temptations of the minor key.

I would like all truths to be borne on Mozart's harmonies, a sound equivalent to the perfume of roses. But since truths have neither tonality nor resonance, an empty soul can also receive them as they are, cold.

✧

Death makes no sense except to people who have passionately loved life. How can one die without having something to part from? Detachment is a negation of both life and death. Whoever has overcome his fear of death has also triumphed over life. For life is nothing but another word for this fear.

Only rich people *experience* death; poor people expect it; no beggar ever died. Only owners die.

Compared to the agony of the rich, that of poor people is like a bed of flowers. Death has gathered into itself all the terrors and sufferings of palaces. To die in luxury is to die a million times.

Beggars don't pass away in their beds and that's why they don't die. One dies only horizontally, through lengthy preparation by means of which death slowly infiltrates life. What regrets could one have, who is not tied to a specific space and its inherent memories in the last hour? Maybe beggars have *chosen* their fate, for by not having any regrets they don't experience the agony that comes from them. Vagrants on the surface of life, they still wander on the surface of death.

✧

Anna Magdalena Bach tells us in her family chronicle that J. S. Bach often meditated on death. Even without her testimony, it is obvious that for Bach preoccupation with death and nostalgia for heaven are sources of the sublime. Mozart has neither one nor the other. That's why his music can be divine, but by no means sublime. I don't know of any musician less cosmic than Mozart.

✧

There is a whole range of melancholy: it begins with a smile and a landscape and ends with the clang of a broken bell in the soul.

✧

While he was composing the *Messiah*, Handel felt as if he were in heaven. He himself confessed that only after finishing it did he realize that he was living on earth. Yet, in spite of this, Handel, compared to Bach, is *of this world*. That which in Bach is *divine* is heroic in Handel. *Terrestrial grandeur* is Handel's signature. The heavens are reflected everywhere in his work: transfiguration *from outside*.

Bach unites Grünewald's dramatic power with Holbein's interiority; Handel, the linear massivity of Dürer with the daring vision of Baldung-Grien. Mozart is a melancholy Botticelli: "Primavera" covered with the dew of tears.

✧

The more you advance in life, the more you realize that you don't learn anything, you just go back in memory. It is as if we reinvent a world in which we once lived. We don't gain anything, we just regain ourselves. Self-identity is reverse evolution. Thus was born the hypothesis of another life, previous to the accident of individuation. Our being imitates an original forgotten vision. What then could be the metaphysical meaning of a saint's existence? Are they haunted by dateless memories which evoke the immediate proximity of God in paradise? Could they be hiding in the depths of their memory the figure of Divinity?

Saints imitate God under the subconscious pressure of their first memory.

For every man, God is his first memory. While going back in memory is beyond an ordinary man's capacity, it becomes the saints' main achievement, although they do not always fully understand the direction of their efforts.

Saintly meditation is an imprisonment in original memory. Divinity is at the absolute limit of memory. That original content is inherited by all, from the beasts of paradise down to us. One reaches the original memory only by jumping over the real content of memory, over time's *contributions*. Why do almost all madmen speak of God or believe themselves to be one? Having lost the actual contents of their memory, their mind has kept intact the original depths of memory. The same with drunkenness. Man gets drunk in order to remember God; maybe he goes mad for similar reasons. But there is no doubt whatsoever that this is his only motivation for wanting to become a saint.

✧

There's nothing precise or definite about saints. They represent an absolute which we should neither embrace nor reject. Any commitment would compromise us. We lose our life if we are for them; we would be in bad standing with the absolute if we were against them. Had we not had them, we would have been freer. How many doubts we would have been spared! How did they come to cross the paths of our lives? In vain do we try to forget agony.

Organ music cannot be contained within the boundaries of the heart, for it is the expression of a sacred *frisson.* The organ is an instrument which makes palpable God's distance from us. Its sound is our apotheosis, and through it we approach him *in* himself.

No matter what we say, the end of all sadness is a swoon into divinity.

Job, the organ's cosmic lamentations, and weeping willows. Open wounds of nature and the soul. The human heart, God's open wound.

Ecstasy replaces sexuality. The mediocrity of the human race is the only plausible explanation for sexuality. As the only mode of coming out of ourselves, sexuality is a temporary salvation from animality. For every being, intercourse surpasses its biological function. It is a triumph over animality. Sexuality is the only gate to heaven. The saints are not a-sexual but trans-sexual. They no longer need the revelations of sexuality. To be a saint means to be always outside yourself. What else would sexuality *add* to this? Sexual orgasm pales beside the saints' ecstatic trance.

The time when the pharaohs built their pyramids is, of all historical epochs, the only one in which I could be at peace with myself—working as a slave. What a formidable thing, to lift slabs of stone under the lash of the whip, but at the same time to foresee the pyramids' triumph in eternity, and even to feel the void being born around them by time's desertion! The least important among the Egyptian slaves was closer to eternity than any European philosopher! For us, the very sky is now our tombstone! The modern world was touched, as if by a curse, by the seduction of finite things!

I love saints for their *passionate naiveté,* which lends their features an expression of childish candor and gratuitous pain. Eyes always half-closed, so that their lids can protect the inner mystery from the indiscretion of external light; a thoughtful smile matching the ambiguity of their gaze; red lips illuminated by the blue of the sky; pale hands stretched for an otherwordly embrace, and that seraphic blue with which Raphael clothes his madonnas, as if it were the essence of their hearts.

Why should they open their eyes on the world when they all have said repeatedly that they only have eyes for Jesus? Ecstasy closes eyes; in it one *is* what one *sees.* That's why it can do away with sight. Bernini grasped this when he sculpted St. Teresa in ecstasy with her eyes barely open. Similarly, Zurbaran, unsurpassed painter of heavenly passions, gave Francis of Assisi a face which his supernatural poise did not deserve.

Mozart makes me regret Adam's sin.

Will there ever be a time when I will quote only God?

❖

Men, even saints, don't have names. Only God bears one. But do we know anything about him other than that he is the source of all despair? God's despair begins where others' end.

✧

Only paradise or the sea could make me give up music.

✧

Dreams of happiness cause me the keenest regrets: Botticelli, Claude Lorrain, Mozart, Watteau, and Corot. Could it be that I am not well-equipped for happiness? Have I only known the melancholy which precedes it and the sadness which follows?

✧

Happiness is a charming pause which I divined in the pastoral elegies of eighteenth-century music. I can only speak about happiness from hearsay.

✧

There are sadnesses which cast in one's soul the shadow of monasteries. Through them, we can begin to understand the saints. Though saints may want to keep us company to the limits of bitterness, they cannot; they abandon us halfway, in our desolation and repentance. Their heart, its axis fixed in God, has a different tilt than ours.

✧

After all the saints' outpourings of love to God, what can we add that will not make us mere epigones? Nonsense? They even used that to express their excessive love. For example, here's the Dominican of Töss, Mezzi Sidwibrin: "My Lord, had you been Mezzi Sidwibrin and I God, I would have wanted you God and myself Mezzi Sidwibrin."

Whoever cannot love him to absurdity might just as well not bother to love him at all. If you speak of God to feel less lonely in your nothingness, he is nothing more than an invention and a pretext for loneliness. The saints knew how to be sad *for* God; for us he is, at most, an outlet for sadness. They were in awe; we cannot be more than *interested*.

One reads the following declaration by Catherine of Siena: "Oh you, abyss of charity, you seem to be mad with love for your creatures, as if you couldn't live without them, though you are Our God. Oh, Eternal Father, oh, fire, abyss of charity, eternal beauty, eternal wisdom, eternal pity, eternal and infinite good, oh, mad with love!" One is stunned by the inexplicable, but also relieved that such excesses preempt the need of a reply. One cannot add anything, except regret for not being able to hate God with a passion equal to this love.

Had there not been any illnesses in the world, there would not have been any saints, for until now there has not been a single healthy one. Saintliness is the cosmic apogee of illness, the transcendental fluorescence of rot. Illnesses have brought the heavens close to earth. Without them, heaven and earth would not have known each other. The need for consolation went further than any illness and, at the point of intersection between heaven and earth, it gave birth to sainthood.

I'm trying to imagine a spaceless world—and all I find is the heart of a saint.

There are people who stylize their own death. For them, dying is merely a question of form. But death is matter and terror. That's why, without avoiding death, one cannot die elegantly.

Why do tall or fat people, once they are grasped by the fear of death, offer such a sinister and discouraging spectacle? In so much matter, death finds a more certain and more congenial nest, and terror grows in direct proportion to the dimensions of matter.

Every time I think about Tolstoy's fear of death, I begin to understand the elephant's fear.

The limit of every pain is an even greater pain.

Acceptance of death was invented by those who tried to flee their fear of death. But without this fear, death is pointless. Death exists only in it and through it. Wisdom born out of a reconciliation with death is the most superficial attitude in front of finality. Even Montaigne was infected with this fear, for otherwise his proud acceptance of the inevitable is inexplicable.

Whoever conquers his fear of death believes himself to be immortal; whoever does not have this fear, *is.* Maybe beings in paradise also died, but not knowing fear they never had the opportunity to die. To fear is to die every minute. Those who do not know fear are like the birds of the sky: they read their destiny in the azure.

Coming after Shakespeare and Dostoevsky, we can no longer be wise. Through them, people have recovered their pain and, reneging on their memory of origins, have begun to take pride in the loss of paradise.

From an objective point of view, all mortals are equidistant from death. We are all subject to death at any moment. From a subjective point of view—the only one that matters—some are so close to it that they almost identify with it, while others have never met it. Objective death makes no sense in Rilke or Novalis. In fact, there is no poet who dies only once.

Ordinary men differ from saints in their attitude toward the body, not in their orientation toward heaven. No man owns heaven, but every saint has a body. Is the body a problem for ordinary men? Only to the extent that it can be sick. Otherwise they carry it unawares. For the saints, though, it becomes a constant obsession.

Ecstasy is an infinite leap beyond the body. Many are the testimonies bringing uncontested proof of the defeat of the body. Saints' confessions are nothing but the record of the struggle of their conscience with their body. But since it is intentional, this conflict lacks drama and reveals nothing, while the *rediscovery of the body* does. Mystical trances sometimes last a long time, go for days on end. The soul is in permanent tension, and the entire being, following in its steps, forgets its adherence to a body. Inner flames refine physical resistance to such an extent that there is nothing left of the body except the immateriality of ecstasy. Once the high intensity of ecstatic trance slows down, the return to the ordinary begins, and with it the surprise of rediscovering a body which has forgotten itself. All saints complain about the recovery of their body, that is, about the fall from ecstasy.

When she was twenty-four, Cristina Ebner had a dream which cannot leave us unmoved. In it, she was pregnant, and her baby was none other than Jesus Christ. Her joy was so great that she would not move for fear of harming the divine baby. After giving birth painlessly, she took him in her arms and showed him to the nuns, saying: "Rejoice with me, for I can't hide my joy any longer, I conceived Jesus and bore him."

Unfortunately for her, she woke up. Had she died then, she would have died of a happiness unknown to any woman.

Her dream was not a nun's dream but a saint's. It is hidden in every saint's heart, all of them: beings pregnant with God.

Cristina Ebner lived from 1277 to 1355. The Middle Ages were pregnant with God.

One Sunday, he said to Cristina: "I come to you like one who is dying of love. I come to you with the desire of a bridegroom at the bed of his bride." In such circumstances it is good to be God, and even more pleasant to be his bride.

"The sensation of being everything and the certitude of being nothing" (Paul Valéry). A poet's conclusion—obligatory for those who have kept company with the saints.

Begging is not the product of poverty. In a perfect state there would be as many beggars as in a historical state. The professional beggar is a permanent feature of life. As long as there will be crossroads, gates, and pity, he will come out of nowhere. Beggars are the perfume of crossroads, the cordiality of gates, the salvation of all charitable people. Without them, pity would dilate like a void in consciousness and, unable to place itself somewhere, it would give way to a sweeping dissatisfaction. It may very well be that pity created begging, or at least they were born together. Social injustice brings to the surface only casual beggars, with no vocation for begging, *fallen* poor folk. The instinctive beggar is a being nobody understands. Charitable people understand him least of all, and besides, they fear him. If I were a beggar, I would not take from anybody. But herein lies the beggar's sublimity: he takes from all. For him, the giver, individually, means nothing. He's only interested in the gesture of bending, the compliment every giver pays him by bowing in front of him. His pride follows the curve of our disdain. The more we bend disdainfully to throw him a farthing, the brighter are his eyes. A beggar would be even happier if we slapped him, for it is his only contact with *man*. Why don't I have a beggar's calling? Truly, one must be born a beggar.

Whoever reads the saints' confessions cannot help thinking that Jesus was sent into the world not so much to save people as to comfort the hearts of women starved for love. Mundane interpretations are not appropriate for saints, but it looks almost certain that had a mortal lover competed with Jesus for the heart of a saint, Our Savior would have remained a simple member of the Trinity.

Jesus was the official lover of saintly women. They did not risk anything by confessing to him all that they had in their heart, and courted no danger in their excess of indiscretion. The saints' longing for love would have given birth to an inner desert had it not been for the omnipresent divine eros, which perfumed their desires and their weaknesses.

Hearts devoid of earthly love are the support of Jesus, his resting place. He's been resting there for two thousand years, caressed by graces he never dreamt of in his manger. From a manger into a saint's heart! Not a mortal evolution.

✧

I'm the Antaeus of despair. Any contact with earth increases my despair. If only I could sleep in God in order to die unto myself!

The only genuine forgetfulness is the sleep in Divinity. When will God close his eyelid over me?

Mechthild of Magdeburg speaking to God: "I bring you my song, more sublime than the mountains, more unfathomable than the seas, higher than the clouds, vaster than the sky."

"What is the name of your song?"

"My heart's desire. I tore it away from the world. I shrank away from myself. I robbed the entire creation. But now I can no longer bear it. Where shall I lay it down?"

"You must put your heart's desire in my heart."

I've known for a long time that tears are the only commentary on saints.

My Lord, I shall dredge tears from the gates of hell and make my home in them. I shall fold your shadows in my twilights. Can it be that God is only a delusion of the heart as the world is one of the mind?

God's advent coincides with the first quiver of loneliness. He finds his place in the emptiness of a tremor. Divine infinity thus equals all the moments of loneliness endured by all beings.

Nobody believes in God—except to avoid the torment of solitary monologue. Is there anyone else to speak to? He seems to welcome any dialogue, and does not resent being the theatrical pretext of our solitary sorrows.

Loneliness without God is sheer madness. At least our ravings end in him, and thus we cure our mind and soul. God is a sort of lightning rod. For God is a good *conductor* of sorrows and disillusions.

Dostoevsky was the last man who tried to save paradise. But he only succeeded in creating a stronger predilection for the Fall. He thus dealt paradise, and our aspirations for it, a final blow.

Dostoevsky was also the last to know Adam before his fall. However, he only succeeded in teaching us the voluptuousness of sin.

We try in vain to canonize Dostoevsky. We shall always fail. Yet I don't know of any saint who would not be proud to unfasten the buckle of his sandal.

The greatest piece of good luck Jesus had was that he died young. Had he lived to be sixty, he would have given us his memoirs instead of the cross. Even today, we would still be blowing the dust off God's unlucky son.

Joseph, the father of Jesus, is the most compromised person in history. The Christians shoved him aside and made him the laughingstock of all men. Had he told the truth at least once, his son would have remained an obscure Jew. The triumph of Christianity originates in a virility that lacked self-esteem. The Virgin Birth originates in the world's piety and one man's cowardice.

When I realized that there was no absolute except in renunciation, I dedicated myself to appearances.

Only the brothel or an angel's tear can free us temporarily from the terror of death.

The Middle Ages were well acquainted with the technique of producing tears, those proofs of ardent passion. To obtain the "gift of tears," prayers were said, and promises of mortification given. Even Thomas Aquinas had this gift, considered the true way of loving God. Formulas for the adoration of God abounded. The Middle Ages were saturated with tears. Their rivers of tears haven't quite dried up even today, and whoever has an ear for pain can still hear their lamentations. Saint Dominic, who had this gift in a big way, would render such woeful sighs at night that the other monks would wake up and join his lamentations.

The Middle Ages expiated Adam's sin, thus making the Renaissance possible.

One day before his conversion, Francis of Assisi was walking along the highway weeping. Thinking he was ill, a man asked him: "What's the matter with you, brother?" "Ah," he answered, "For the love of Christ, I should not be ashamed of going around the world like this grieving for my Savior's agony."

The Middle Ages, having exhausted the contents of eternity, gave us the right to love transitory things.

The whole of Christianity is mankind's fit of crying, of which only salty and bitter traces are now left to us.

Anonymous books entitled *The Art of Dying* appeared towards the end of the Middle Ages. They were incredibly popular. Would such a book move anyone today?

What separates us from antiquity and the Middle Ages is the fact that we no longer know how to prepare ourselves for death. No one cultivates death *in* himself any longer, it happens *over and above* him.

The ancients knew how to die. Contempt for death was born with them. But their contempt came from knowledge. Their ideal was to rise spiritually above death. For us, death is a painful and frightening *surprise.* Hence our terror and its drama. No ancient was ever surprised by death, and thus they could afford to smile at its approach, a fact which astonishes us. They were so persuaded of death's *inevitability* that they invented an elaborate art of dying. Though we may know this art, it cannot help us.

The Middle Ages lived in even greater intimacy with death than antiquity. Both, however, are united in a common belief in a complex system of preparations that would allow a more successful, more organic death. That belief separates them from us. The Middle Ages experienced death with unique intensity. Through meditation and the "art of dying," death became an intimate part of being. Thus people died "legally"; death had its own form, its own statutes. For us, it only signifies incessant harassment, from which we would like to escape. We take comfort in fear. I don't think that one could find, either in antiquity or the Middle Ages, a single man who would try to play hooky from death. For an ancient philosopher or a medieval monk, "there is no way out" would make a constant theme for meditation. We would rather die without having any such thing as death.

✧

One can only think horizontally. It is almost impossible to conceive of eternity from a vertical position. Animals may well have evolved to the rank of men when they started to walk upright, but *consciousness* was born in moments of freedom and laziness. As you lie stretched out on the ground, your eyes staring at the sky above, the separation between you and the world opens up like a gap—without which consciousness is not possible. Not a single thought is born standing; horizontal immobility is an essential condition for meditation. True, no happy thoughts are born thus. But meditation is an expression of nonparticipation, and therefore has no tolerance for being. History is the product of the verti-

cal line, whereas nothingness comes from the horizontal
line.

The church has always regarded the saints' *private revelations,* in which they mix God with intimate
circumstances of their own lives, with great caution and
reserve. But these revelations are precisely the most sincere as well as the closest to our hearts. Uncensored
celestial visions have a savory naiveté. Thus for example,
Jesus calls Angela da Foligno by her nickname, Lella,
and as he shows her his wounds, he whispers: "All of
these are for you." Again, speaking to Margaret of Cortona, he says "I love no one on earth more than you."

It's true that these are not official revelations; but
they constitute the delicious madness of sainthood.

Didn't Jesus whisper one day to Angela, "of all the
saints in paradise, you are my only love"? It is a truly
private revelation; we cannot interfere with it without
provoking divine jealousy.

The saints' existence is a continuous suspension of
time. That's why we can understand them only through
our predilection for eternity.

According to Jakobus de Voragine, the angels' task is
to stamp the memory of Christ's agony onto the souls
of men. And I had thought them agents of heavenly
forgetfulness!

Mechthild of Magdeburg inscribed her revelations on
the wings of angels. Her enthusiasm inspires me with
such a longing for self-destruction that I wish to be pul-
verized like stardust!

Saintly women have stolen my soul and hidden it under big mounds of stardust. From those heights, I would like to cry into their hearts.

God has exploited all our inferiority complexes, starting with our disbelief in gods.

"And you would have kissed my soul." Thus speaks God to Mechthild's soul in her *Dialogues.* Finally, some reserve and decency in divine eroticism!

One takes the measure of consciousness from its cosmic expansion. If, once your spirit has bent over it, you still remain anchored in the world, it means that you have missed your way, entangled in cosmic paths. Whoever has not exhausted the world in his inner strife will never reach God. God exists at the limit of consciousness. When we have devoured the world and remain alone, God appears from behind the screen of Nothingness like a last temptation.

Christianity is too profound to last any longer. Its centuries are numbered. How could man have survived for so long so many final questions served up to him in an official way? Man's rare deliriums have become state religion. That the abyss of Christianity has not completely corrupted man is to me the only proof of his vocation for metaphysics.

But man can no longer endure the terror of final questions. Christianity has legalized anxiety, and has kept man under pressure to such an extent that a few thousand years of relaxation will be needed to revive a being devastated by the invasion of so many heavens.

✧

Christianity—a real avalanche of metaphysical indiscretions—has introduced death, suffering, Jesus, and God into men's everyday life, into their politics, their business, their gains and losses. Hence many crises of consciousness are piling up one after another into an architectonics of despair. The Christian demon has woven its nest in money, in sexuality, in love. It has caused humanity so much trouble, that from now on superficiality should undoubtedly be looked upon as a virtue! This demon has pierced our hearts with a cross from which *we* should be hanging, if we want to expiate Christianity through Christian sacrifice. Yet all attempts to free ourselves are vain, for we can never forget its *décor,* namely, the saints. After we had hated Christianity for some time, it would send its saints after us, they would start pursuing us, and, precisely at the moment when we were more certain that we had forgotten all about the agonistic passion, whose poison has spread over centuries, we would again stumble over the saints, and our corpses would fall into their outstretched arms.

We would have been quite happy had we remained simple human beings. But we ended up Christians. Could we still retrace our steps?

Christianity was not the way to surpass our humanity. It has made so much propaganda for just *one* God that we are left with no hope whatsoever.

✧

Since the Renaissance, nobody has known *resignation.* Lack of resignation is modern man's tragic aura. The ancients submitted to their fate. No modern man is humble enough to be resigned. Nor are we familiar with contempt for life. We are not wise enough *not* to love it with infinite agony.

The ancients did not make so much of their suffering. This, however, is not the case with us, for we rebel against pain.

Angels *see* everything but *know* nothing. They are illiterates of perfection. They didn't even have enough curiosity to listen to the serpent's temptations. Nor did they ask Adam about the cause of his dismissal. Yet how good they would have looked next to man! Those among the angels who fell, did so *individually*, as traitors. The legions of their followers, however, remained ignorant of temptation. They still watch over us, without understanding us. Neither did we understand anything at the time when we were together in God. Now at least we understand the angels through memory and the hope of return. Their understanding of us was limited to their presentiment of a fall. Do they ever have forebodings, I wonder? I can't forgive the angel with the sword who did not imitate Adam, and would not save his nation through desertion. Adam's fall is paradise's only historical fact.

✧

I often wonder why saints instituted the cult of angels, who are after all their competitors for heavenly glory. Certainly, it was a political mistake, betraying a surprising lack of foresight! Aren't the gates of heaven open to them even without the angels' intercession? Saints may very well be fallen angels who have regained grace. In that case, paradise is for them a more recent memory, which they remember more intensely, making the flame of their desire more fervent. Could this be the reason for their heavenly aspirations? Saints look like angels who have known agony, and therefore knowledge.

The saints' obsession: fighting illness with *illness.*

When music sweeps over us like a wave of mournful happiness, we long for a sweet-smelling death. The saints hold so much music in themselves that they alone can resist the dissolution of the body. Their corpses do not stink. Could I ever hold so much music as never to die? There are minuets after which one could not rot.

Only musical ecstasy makes me feel immortal. Oh, those clear days when your heart borrows color from the sky, and deep sonorities revive memories from beyond the horizon! It will be in vain then to try and shed tears for time.

A heart without music is like beauty without melancholy.

Wine has brought men closer to God than theology. But it's been a long time since sad drunkards (are there any other types?) have shamed the hermits.

Jesus came to Catherine of Siena during one of her ecstasies and, opening the left side of her body, took her heart out. For days afterwards, she kept telling everyone that she was living without a heart. She assured those who doubted her that it was possible, for God could do anything. But then, as she was praying alone in a chapel, she saw his figure in a beam of heavenly light with a heart in his hand. Trembling, she fell to the ground. Jesus came closer and, opening her left side again, placed in it the heart he was holding. Then he said: "You see, dearest girl, as I once took your heart, now I give you mine to live with."

Swooning saints have a moving charm. They prove that we cannot have revelations in a vertical position, that we cannot *stand* on our feet to face the ultimate truth. Swooning provokes such wild voluptuousness that a man cognizant of negative joys has a hard time deciding whether to fall or not.

Weininger used to say that epilepsy was the criminal's last solitude. Having no more ties with the world, all he has left is the fall.

The saints' swooning is no less a breaking of their ties with the world. But they fall into heaven.

There comes a moment in life when one places everything in relation to God. Anything less seems too little. Yet the fear that God may no longer be topical sometimes grabs you, and relating everything to him seems useless. The transience of the ultimate principle—a logically absurd idea, yet present in consciousness—fills you with strange terror. Could God be just a *fashion* of the soul, a fleeting passion of history?

Some people still wonder if life has meaning. In fact, it all comes down to knowing whether it is *bearable.* Then "problems" cease and decisions begin.

God's greatest advantage is that one can say or think anything about him. The less you connect your thoughts, abandoning them to contradictions, the more you risk coming near the truth. God benefits from the peripheries of logic.

Shakespeare and Dostoevsky leave you with an insufferable regret: for having been neither a saint nor a criminal, the two best forms of self-destruction.

✧

The saints were uneducated. Why, then, do they write so well? Is it only inspiration? They have *style* whenever they describe God. It's easy to write from divine whispers, with one's ear glued to his mouth. Their works have a superhuman simplicity. But they cannot be called writers, since they do not describe reality. The world won't accept them because it does not see itself in their work.

✧

One can know a man only by the level to which music has risen in his soul. But I'm interested only in those submerged in music, so I have to do without knowledge of other people.

There are musical souls that have no musical education. We are born with a number of vibrations which our sadness brings into relief. We carry within us all the music we have never heard in our life, which lies at the bottom of the abyss of memory. All that is musical in us is *memory.* When we did not have a *name,* we must have heard *everything.* Music exists only as remembrance of paradise and of the Fall.

Everything must have been *once.* That's why life seems to me like a ghostly undulation. History does not repeat itself; yet it seems as if our lives are caught in the reflections of a past world, whose delayed echoes we prolong. Memory is an argument not only against time but also against this world. It half uncovers the probable worlds of the past, crowning them with a vision of paradise. Regrets spring from the nadir of memory.

Regression in memory makes one a metaphysician; delight in its origins, a saint.

The answer saintly women gave whenever their parents begged them to marry was invariably the same: they could not marry because they had promised Jesus their maidenhood. The wrenching truth is that Jesus does not deserve so many mad renunciations. Whenever I think about the infinity of suffering to which the saints' perverse transcendence has led, the agony of Jesus strikes me as merely sad. The cross broke apart and fell into the saints' souls, and its nails bore into their hearts all their life, not for just a few hours on a hill. The ultimate cruelty was that of Jesus: leaving an inheritance of bloodstains on the cross.

Saints may very well talk about the *delights* of the cross, but why can't they be sincere and speak also of its *poison?* I am trying to imagine noble, superb, charming Magdalena of Pazzi, who under the curse of divine inspiration imprisoned herself in a monastery, and who would, in moments of spiritual crisis and satanic temptation, tie herself to a cross like a condemned woman. So many young lives were crucified because they were born of eternity's hysteria, and followed the heavenly example of a demi-God! Jesus must have a very heavy conscience if he has even an inkling of his responsibility in the face of so much suffering. Heavy red and black crosses will rise from the saints' inhuman suffering on the Day of the Last Judgment to punish the Son, Dealer in Pain.

✧

Had all moments that are not ecstasy been indifferent and insignificant, sainthood would have been a priceless gift. Yet they are not merely dull, they also have a cold, uninterrupted bitterness which dries up the soul and renders it incapable of love. "Dryness of the soul" is the term commonly used by saints to describe this obscure aspect of their condition. They request grace as a liberation from such a state. Whenever their soul is dry, they invoke love. Could their souls be dry only from an absence of love? The saints are mistaken when they attribute their inner void to lack of love. They know physiology only as a supplement of the sky. If they knew they were paying with the dryness of their soul for the vibrations of ecstasy, a cowardly fear would grab them in front of God, and they would not seek new encounters! Everywhere around ecstasy, I see only ruins. As long as we are in ecstasy we are not in ourselves, and our being is nothing but the ruin of immemorial time.

✧

Saint Aldegunda, a descendant of the Frankish kings, gave early signs of a heavenly vocation. Once, as she was lost in meditation, a voice whispered to her: "Do not look for a groom other than the Son of God." Fatal words, since from that moment she fell prey to Jesus. At thirteen, the king of England's son asked to marry her. She rejected him, saying that her whole heart belonged to a lover who surpassed all the sons of the earth both in beauty and riches. Her parents' pleading was in vain; she preferred to die rather than lose the virginity she had promised to the heavenly Don Juan. After her parents' death, she became even more determined not to marry. As the English prince would not give up on her, Aldegunda ran away from her parents' castle to a monastery. Coming to a river she could not cross, she saw the prince in hot pursuit catching up with her. Then an angel appeared and helped her across. Thus this royal victim of Jesus ended her days in a monastery.

This seventh-century drama is neither unique nor extraordinary. It tells us, however, that every saintly woman is an Ophelia, only more passionate, for Jesus is not so blasé a lover as Hamlet.

Shall we also remember here Saint Kunigunda who on her wedding day made her husband swear chastity unto death? In palaces, Jesus has wreaked more havoc than in huts.

The closer I am to the saints, the farther I am from him, and when I feel human pity for saintly women, I definitely hate him.

Pascal is a saint without a temperament.

Nietzsche's greatest merit is that he knew how to defend himself from saintliness. What would have become of him had he let loose his natural impulses? He would have been a Pascal with all the saints' madnesses.

As long as one believes in philosophy, one is healthy; sickness begins when one starts to think.

All great conversions are born from the sudden revelation of life's meaninglessness. Nothing could be more moving or more impressive than this sudden apprehension of the void of existence.

Rancé reformed the order of the Trappists after the unexpected death of his lover. Margaret of Cortona's excessive penitence was due to a similar experience. For years, she had been living far from her family with a noble lover. Once, when he had been away for awhile, she went out to meet him on the day of his return. At a certain turning of the road, her dog jumped at her, tore at her clothes, and ran towards a pile of wood behind which his master lay dead, already putrefied. He had been killed and hidden away on the day of his departure. "Where could his soul be now?" she asked herself, and her suffering at this awful sight changed the course of her life on the spot. Remorse drove her to the limits of penitence. This unhappy saint tortured herself daily so cruelly that she swooned every moment.

Other saints experienced the revelation of *vanitas mundi* in less dramatic but more continuous ways. They were especially gifted for emptiness because they had the soul of a singer of psalms with all its heavenly sweetness.

All saints are sick, but luckily not all sick people are saints. Thus for the saints the end of suffering is the loss of grace. Sickness brings grace, for it nourishes otherworldly passions. Through sickness we understand the saints, and through them, the heavens. Sickness is not ultimate knowledge for everybody. For ordinary mortals, it is only a *mediated* knowledge.

Blue skies make us sadder than gray skies because they offer us hopes which we do not have the courage to entertain. Whereas a gray sky is a tomb without alternative. Blue is a soothing color for melancholy; it is neutral towards divinity. When God's call breaks through the azure, we would rather have heavy black clouds. They allow us the freedom of feeling abandoned without hope. Couldn't we live without a sky?

✧

Our lack of pride belittles death. Christianity taught us to lower our eyes—to look *down*—so that death would find us peaceful and meek. Two thousand years of training accustomed us to a quiet, modest, and sure death. We die *down*. We do not have the courage to look at the sun at the last moment.

If we cannot combine the elegance of an Athenian ephebe with the passions of a conquistador, this same gravitational death is in store for us too. We shall then expire quietly in the shadow cast by our lowered eyes. Oh, but to die with muscles strained like a runner waiting for the starting signal, head thrown back, braving space and conquering death, full of pride and the illusion of force! I often dream of an indiscreet death, in *full sight* of infinity!

✧

Of all human beings, the saints are the least lonely when they die. They are always attended at death either by Jesus or by angels. They who have sought loneliness breathe their last in public. The destiny of a simple mortal is infinitely more bitter since he dies without either heavenly or earthly help, without the cowardly support of dialogue! Whenever their end drew near, the saints turned themselves in and died peacefully, sure of their ultimate destination. But what about all the others, the eternal lepers of this earth, their eyes downcast, looking at the dust under their feet, their soul blown away like dust? How can they die without the refreshing comfort of some little hope? When I think of all the agonies on this earth, I know there are souls which could not be lifted by cohorts of angels, so heavy they will not be able to rise at the Last Judgment, frozen in the barrenness of their own curses. Only light souls can be saved: those whose weight will not break the wings of angels.

✧

People usually do not distinguish between those who are born saints and those who become saints. But it is one thing to see the light of day when you are already loaded with grace, and another to pay dearly for it, and win it step by step. Born saintliness is easy and without responsibility; the saint is only a tool of grace, an unconscious organ of perfection. I dread to think of the saints *without talent,* those who have worked hard for heavenly grace, and paid for it with the sweat of their body and soul. They are more numerous. They owe everything to suffering. The others, the privileged, true owners of the azure, do not go beyond a certain inclination towards suffering, and do not use it more than as a pretext. The talent for saintliness helps you sneak

adroitly through the course of suffering. But most saints
have lain themselves across the path of sufferings, and
not a single one has failed to hit them.

✦

Could saints have a will to power? Is their world imperialistic? The answer is yes, but one must take into
account the change of direction. While we waste our
energy in the struggle for temporary gains, their great
pride makes them aspire to absolute possession. For
them, the space to conquer is the sky, and their weapon,
suffering. If God were not the limit of their ambition,
they would compete in ultimates, and each would speak
in the name of yet another infinity. Man is forever a
proprietor. Not even the saints could escape this mediocrity. Their madness has divided up heaven in unequal
portions, each according to the pride they take in their
sufferings. The saints have redirected imperialism vertically, and raised the earth to its supreme appearance,
the heavens.

✦

Only by forgetting everything can we truly remember.
A weak memory reveals to us the world before time. By
gradually emptying our memory, we detach ourselves
from time. That is why during sleepless nights we relive
ancestral fears, worlds that we do not remember, but
which surprise us like memory. Such nights do not do
away with the actual content of our memory (our history), but they take us on a path winding backwards
through time. Insomnia is regression to origins and the
beginning of individuation. It thins out time to the
point of mere optical illusion; it expels us from tempo-

rality and forces on us the last of memories, i.e., the very first ones. In the melodious dissolution of insomnia, we exhaust our past. And then it seems as if we have died along with all of time.

The more time has disappeared from one's memory, the closer one is to mysticism.

Paradise is not possible without a defective memory. The healthier memory is, the more it adheres to the world. The archeology of memory unearths documents from other worlds at the expense of this one.

When I think of the loneliness of nights, and the agony of this loneliness, I long to wander on roads unknown to saints. Where to, where to? There are abysses even outside the soul.

I must have lived other lives. If not, whence so much dread? Previous lives are the only explanation for dread. Only the Orientals understood the soul. They were before us and they will be after us. Why did we moderns suppress the memory of our wanderings, admitting only *one* time? Every moment we must atone for infinite becoming. Have we reached the limit of dread? We shall end our lives only at the end of dread.

Becoming is nothing more than a cosmic sigh. We are the wounds of nature, and God is doubting Thomas.

Compared to philosophers, saints know nothing. Yet they know everything. Compared to Aristotle, any saint is an illiterate. What makes us then believe that we might learn more from the latter? Because all of the philosophers put together are not worth a single saint. Philosophy has no answers. Compared to philosophy, saintliness is an *exact science.* It gives us precise answers to questions that philosophers do not even dare consider. Its method is suffering and its goal is God. Since it is neither practical nor easy, men place it in the domain of the fantastic and worship it from afar. They keep philosophy closer the better to despise it, and they treat philosophers with respectful indifference. In this, ordinary people prove to be intelligent. For whatever is valid in philosophy comes from its borrowings from religion and mystical revelations. In itself, philosophy, like the rest of culture, is nothing.

Philosophers are cold-blooded. There is no heat except near God. That's why the Siberia of our souls clamors for saints.

Nothing easier than shedding philosophical inheritance, for the roots of philosophy do not go farther than our insecurities, whereas those of saintliness *surpass* even sufferings. Therefore, could I ever forget them? Skepticism is philosophy's last courage. Beyond it, there is only chaos. It is true that the freedom of the spirit attained by the Greek skeptics could provoke the jealousy of the mystics, but this unique development was compromised by modern scientific relativism. After all, science is nothing more than the sum of vulgar doubts for an educated stupidity. There is no science except at the antipodes of the spirit.

A philosopher is saved from mediocrity either through skepticism or mysticism, the two forms of despair in front of knowledge. Mysticism is an escape from knowledge, and skepticism is knowledge without hope. In either instance, the world is *not* a solution.

✧

The only people I envy are the confessors and the biographers of saintly women, not to mention their secretaries. If only we knew all that Peter Olafsson did *not* say about Saint Birgitta, or Heinrich von Halle about Mechthild of Magdeburg, Raymond of Capua about Catherine of Siena, Brother Arnold about Angela da Foligno, John Marienwerder about the Blessed Dorothea of Montau, and Brentano about Catherine Emmerich, we would be privy to all their secrets, all those forbidden details which would enhance the strange aura of saintliness. If only we could be near them in their moments of doubt, and delight in their agony with a perfection of sadism! Rejoice because you cannot soften their fate, and turn their tears into a source of voluptuous pleasure!

What would it be like to be the chronicler of a monastery, to keep a diary of crises and illuminations, staining its pages with the bloody torments of budding saints? I have often dreamt myself the chronicler of these fallings from heaven to earth, the intimate knower of the ardors in their hearts, the historian of God's insomniacs.

✧

Through their names, Diodata degli Ademari and Diana d'Andolo ascended to heaven. Piety adds a transcendent perfume to the beauty of the name. Saints' names have the sensual feeling of other worlds. So many saintly women justify their otherwordliness by the sound of their name.

The Church was wrong to canonize so few women saints. Its misogyny and stinginess make me want to be more generous. Any woman who sheds tears for love in loneliness is a saint. The Church has never understood that saintly women are made of God's tears.

Plato deplores the fact that no poet has ever sung the space extending beyond the sky, nor ever will. Could it be that Plato was a total stranger to music? How could he then know that madness is one of man's greatest blessings? Or was his assertion merely accidental? It may very well have been, since he confessed that the gods often whispered in his ear.

Our suffering cannot be anything but futile and satanic. Any poem by Baudelaire says more to modern man than the saints' sublime excesses. Abandoning ourselves to despair as if to drinking or dancing, we have lost interest in a scale of perfection achieved through suffering. Modern man is not opposed to saints through his superficiality but rather through what is uncontrollable in his condition, his wallowing in a tragic orgy, his sliding into forever-renewed delusions. Lack of training in the selection of sadness has led to modern man's inability to resist himself. If God shows himself through sensations, so much the better! We shall no longer suffer the inhuman discipline of revelation. Saints are completely out-of-date, and only one who despises Becoming can still be interested in them.

✧

The only interesting philosophers are the ones who have stopped thinking and have begun to search for happiness. In this way, twilight philosophies are born. They are more comforting than religions because they free us from authority. With Epicurus, one's thoughts sway in the cool breeze of a palm tree, and the sky looks like an open fan fluttering to preserve the freshness of doubts. The twilight philosophers—so full of shadows that they no longer believe in anything—embrace you like a sea cradling your drowned body. Their smile suggests a welcome therapy: *all is allowed.* Those balmy, dizzying doubts that make us want to die of happiness in the shadow of a smile, what a relief after the saints' excesses and restrictions!

Socrates, in spite of his demons, and Aristotle, in spite of his encyclopedia, are less interesting than the last skeptic at the end of the Greco-Roman era, who from its twilight spread the shadows of doubt over the entire world of Antiquity. It was easy to be Socrates, Democritus, or even Heraclitus. All one needed was genius, because Greek thinking required a certain form of originality, following a specific logic of problem-solving. Problems *sought* you out, and if you were a genius, you solved them: there was no other way. Then someone else would come along, born with different problems, which were not yours.

But once these problems are exhausted, what use is genius?

Skepticism is genius surprised by the absence of problems and the void of reality. Only the Ancients knew how to be skeptical, only those who belonged to the Alexandrian period. They doubted with style. Their reflections on the world were gravely autumnal, expressing a disabused happiness, a warm abstention that bore no grudge. Skepticism, delicate shadow of the spirit, blooming in the twilight of cultures, has lent philosophical concepts poetic grace and charming dilettantism.

How could the Greek skeptic, who had behind him the entire body of Ancient thought, and who was being assailed by Oriental religions, still decide among divergent philosophies, all equally justifiable? Thus was born the pleasure of wandering among ideas and worlds, so characteristic of Alexandrian epochs. In just one life you can exhaust centuries or even millennia of history. Homer and Epicure coexist at this time, and so do Judaic messianism and the Persian religion: an eclecticism which took a joyful pride in the expansion of the soul and was painfully disappointed with the delusions of culture. Alexandrianism is a *paradise of bitterness.*

Philosophy is a corrective against sadness. Yet there still are people who believe in the *profundity* of philosophy!

The philosophers' sole merit is that they *sometimes* felt ashamed of being men. Plato and Nietzsche are exceptions: they were *always* ashamed. The former wanted to take us out of this world, the latter out of ourselves. Even the saints could learn something from them. Thus the honor of philosophy was saved!

The saints' goodness is repulsive. It is like a sickly discoloration combined with an emasculation of being. Their supreme indifference is off-putting.

The only explanation for the creation of the world is God's fear of solitude. In other words, our role is to *amuse* Our Maker. Poor clowns of the absolute, we forget that we act out a tragedy to enliven the boredom of one spectator whose applause has never reached a mortal ear. Solitude weighs on God so much that he invented the saints as partners in dialogue.

I can stand up to God only by confronting him with another solitude. Without my solitude I would be nothing more than another clown.

There are hearts into which even God cannot look without losing his innocence.

Sadness begins on this side of creation, where God has never been. For, confronted with the human heart, how could he have maintained his poise?

They say the saints' corpses do not stink. One more proof that saints do not belong to this world. The corpses of saintly women even give off a scented odor. There are perfumes in the air evoking the agony of saints which, if inhaled, send you into a trance. Many a time have I closed the eyes of dying holy maidens!

We moderns have discovered hell inside ourselves and that is our good fortune. For what would have become of us if we had only had hell's external and historical representations? Two thousand years of fear would have driven us to suicide. Saint Hildegard's description of the Last Judgment makes one hate all heavens and hells, and rejoice that they are only subjective visions. Psychology is both our salvation and our superficiality. According to a Christian legend, the world was born when the Devil yawned. For us moderns, the accident of this world is nothing more than a psychological error.

What better proof that music is not human than the fact that it has never awakened in me visions of hell? Not even funeral marches could do it. Hell is an *actuality*; therefore, we can only remember paradise. Had we known hell in our immemorial past, wouldn't we sigh now after a *Hell Lost?*

Music is the archeology of memory. Its excavations have not discovered anywhere a hell that precedes memory.

Why is it that every time we try to break through the physical matter that fetters our spiritual effervescence, all our efforts are in vain? Only music defeats matter on this earth. A few airy tunes, a melodious breeze blowing from the soul, have the power of a blowtorch, melting all our material shackles in its intense flames.

✧

One begins to know solitude when one hears the silence of things. Then one knows the secret buried in the stone and reawakened in the plant, Nature's hidden as well as open ways. The odd thing about solitude is that it knows no inanimate objects. All objects have a language which we can decipher only in total silence. There is a burning solitude in which all is *life.* The spirit is asleep in nature, and I would like to interpret the dreams of plants.

Shadows too have their life of mystery. There haven't been enough poets in this world, for so many things have remained undisclosed, estranged from their own meaning!

✧

Music is everything. God himself is nothing more than an acoustic hallucination.

✧

With time suspended, consciousness exhausts itself in the perception of space, and we acquire an eleatic disposition. Universal stillness does away with our memories in a moment of eternity. Space takes hold of us to such extent that the world seems useless, endless expectation. That is when the longing for stillness possesses us, for space is a tantalizing quiver of immobility.

✧

I am bent over under the weight of a curse called eternity, a poison of youth, a balm only for corrupt hearts. A man's good health can be measured in direct proportion to his hatred for and resistance to eternity. The saints' illness is their penchant for it.

When the void of time gives birth to eternity, one burns with religious courage. The emptying of time, whether out of boredom or dread, throws one into a vibrant nothingness, full of vague promises. No saint could find eternity in the world. Crossing the inner desert constitutes the first step toward saintliness.

God nestles in spiritual voids. He covets inner deserts, for God, like an illness, incubates at the point of least resistance. A harmonious being cannot believe in God. Saints, criminals, and paupers have launched him, making him available to all unhappy people.

At times, when I am seething with cosmic hatred against all otherwordly agents, I would submit them to unspeakable tortures in order to save appearances. A secret voice whispers to me incessantly that if I were to live among saints I would need to carry a dagger. A St. Bartholomew's massacre among angels would delight me immensely. I would have these preachers of desertion from the world hung by their tongues, and thrown on a bed of lilies. Why do we lack the prudence to suppress all otherwordly vocations early on, and to close all windows to heaven forever?

How can one not hate the angels, the saints, and God, that entire band from paradise which fuels such a passionate longing for other shelters and other temptations? Heaven irritates me. In its Christian guise, it drives me to despair.

In the world of feeling, tears are the criterion for truth. Tears, but not crying. There is a disposition toward tears which manifests itself through an *internal* avalanche. Whoever has cried only outwardly remains ignorant of their origin and meaning. There are connoisseurs of tears who have never actually cried, and yet they try hard not to provoke a cosmic flood!

Solitude is like the ravaged bottom of a tumultuous sea where rapidly unfurling waves threaten to destroy the barriers of our being.

Only poetry lovers are irresponsible and lax with the spirit. One feels that *all is allowed* each time one reads a poem. Not having to account for anything to anyone (except to himself), a poet leads you nowhere. To understand poets is a curse, for one learns then that there is nothing to lose.

There isn't anything more soothing than the poetry of the saints. But they fatally limit their poetic genius by addressing an interlocutor, who is, in most cases, God. Though sacred, poetry is a godless frisson. Had the saints only known that their appeal to God weakened their lyricism, they would have renounced saintliness and become poets. We would have had then less philanthropy in the world, but more freedom and irresponsibility! Saintliness knows only *freedom in God.* As for mortals, they know only poetic license.

✧

The visions of saintly women have an added plus of femininity, complete with all its charming vanities. Thus Catherine of Ricci's "The Bedecking of the Soul" is a transposition into spiritual terms of all the earthly splendors treasured by a vain and beautiful woman. On the third of May, 1542, during a divine trance, Catherine saw herself surrounded by Thomas Aquinas, Saint Martha, Saint Catherine of Siena, Mary Magdalene, and Saint Agnes. They were adorning her with pearls and other precious stones, and sprinkling rich, exotic perfumes on her. Her necklaces, her red cape, her multicolored sash, the precious stones, all symbolized superior and inferior virtues. Paradise flowers, symbol of pure desires, enveloped her neck, and her crown of pearls symbolized the most rare and saintly virtues.

Thus bedecked, and accompanied by the saints, she was taken to Jesus who embraced her, kissed her, held her fast in his arms. Her mind must have been engulfed in a frenzy of light and vanity to project such splendid shadows!

✧

If truth were not boring, science would have done away with God long ago. But God as well as the saints is a means to escape the dull banality of truth.

✧

Saint Teresa is a synonym for heart.

✧

Jesus spoke thus to Margaret-Mary: "My daughter, your soul shall be my haven of peace on earth, and your heart, a bed of delights for my divine love!" Her comment: "Ever since, my soul has been quiet. I fear that I might trouble the peace of my Savior!"

While praying before the wounds of Jesus, especially his open, bleeding heart, Saint Mechthild heard him say: "Come into my heart and travel across it. Take its measure, in it you shall find the measure of my love for you and of my desire to save you for eternity. Come, to you belongs all the good you shall find in my heart!"

Saintliness interests me for the delirium of self-aggrandizement hidden beneath its meekness, its will to power masked by goodness. Saints have used their deficiencies to their best advantage. Yet their megalomania is undefinable, strange, and moving. Those who can only live in the heart of Jesus and talk only to God are never *vanquished.* Whence then our compassion for them? We no longer believe in them. *We only admire their illusions.* Hence our compassion.

Who can identify with precision the moment in which paradise resurfaces in our consciousness? A weakness in our bones, a subtle sickness invading our flesh, and we collapse in a voluptuous inner swoon. Matter, touched by ecstasy, disperses in a shimmering light, and everything vibrates with such alluring intensity that we fall on our knees, our arms raised imploringly, like lovers or hermits. The stars or the azure hurt our adoring gaze. So much immateriality is offensive! The ecstasy of dissolution and *inactuality* in life are the conditions for the *actualization* of paradise.

You are alive only when you live by the skin of your teeth.

After great pain, a voluptuous feeling comes, as of infinite happiness. I agree with the saints on this point: he who has sipped the cup of suffering to its last dregs can no longer be a pessimist.

While men are haunted by the memory of paradise, angels are tormented by longing for this world.

The saints complain of a moment in which they cease to think. There has been some learned talk about the total dissolution of conceptual thinking during moments of ecstasy, but hardly any about that state of vagueness which, though not yet on the plane of ecstasy, eradicates thought. The saints interest me precisely for this state of spiritual vagueness. That the flame of ecstasy annihilates any kind of intellectual activity is relatively easy to imagine. Much harder to seize is the chaotic dream that rises from spiritual vagueness. No philosophy can explain such moments. Philosophers insist on making distinctions, and leave us behind without a clue, so desperately hopeless that we cling to saints like a drowning man to the shipwreck of his boat.

Isn't there enough suffering in the world? It seems not, to judge from the saints who excel in self-torture. Saintliness cannot exist without the voluptuousness of pain and a perverse refinement of suffering. Saintliness is a celestial vice.

I can't forgive the saints for having undertaken their great feats without first tasting the *plenitude of the ephemeral.* And I will not forgive them for not having shed a single tear of gratitude for things that pass.

Every time I feel a passionate longing for the earth, for all that is born and dies, every time I hear the call of the ephemeral, I must protect God from my hatred. I spare him out of immemorial cowardice. Yet I think of the revenge of transitory things and I fear for his safety.

Without our intimation of the approaching night which we call God, life would be a cheerful twilight.

Were heaven and earth to disappear, the saints' tears would still endure. Out of light and tears, a new world would be born, in which we could heal our memories.

Music induces heavenly visions in all mystic souls. Marianna of Quito, for example, when asked to play the guitar by her friend, Petronilla, fell into a trance after strumming just a few notes. An hour later, she came back to her senses and, with tears running down her cheeks, she sighed: "My dear Petronilla, if you only knew how many wonderful things there are in heaven!"

You are lost if saints don't disgust you. Saintliness is systematic insomnia, the heart perpetually awake. Suppressing sleep is a confessed ambition: thus Peter of Alcantara, whom Teresa of Avila knew personally, and who was acclaimed as a saint while still alive, for forty years did not sleep for more than one and a half hour each night. Fasting and sleeplessness are required conditions for sainthood.

Saintliness is a negative sort of perfection. I love life too much to attain it. Because of my reserves of health, I remain a heavenly interloper. There are illnesses that can only be treated with a good dose of divinity, but I prefer the alleviation of pain provided by earthly tranquilizers. I don't have the gift of infinite joy and pain which used to throw Saint Teresa of Avila and Angela da Foligno into ecstasy. I am healthy, that is I can stand and talk about God, not fall down at the very thought of him. What a heavy price one must pay for one's health!

Whenever I think of austere solitude, I see gray shadows cast in deserts by monasteries, and I try to understand those sad intervals of piety, their mournful boredom. The passion for solitude, which engenders "the monastic absolute"—that all-consuming longing to bury oneself in God—grows in direct proportion to the desolation of the landscape. I see glances broken by walls, untempted hearts, sadness devoid of music. Despair born out of implacable deserts and skies has led to an aggravation of saintliness. The "aridity of consciousness," about which the saints complain, is the psychic equivalent of external desert. The initial revelation of any monastery: everything is nothing. Thus begin all mysticisms. It is less than one step from nothing to God, for God is the *positive* expression of nothingness.

One can never comprehend the temptation of solitude and of despair without first having knowledge of the temporal and spatial vacuum in a monastic cell. I think of Spanish monasteries in particular, where so many kings sheltered their melancholies and so many saints cultivated their madness. Spain symbolizes the pitiless desert of the soul. Its merit is not only to have saved the absurd for the world but also to have demonstrated that man's normal temperature is madness. Thus saints come naturally to this people which has done away with the distance between heaven and earth. Were God a cyclops, Spain would be his eye.

One must think of God day and night in order to wear him out, to turn him into a cliché. We can free ourselves from him only by appealing to him incessantly, in order to tire ourselves out and make him superfluous. The persistence with which God settles himself in our inner space will end by nullifying him. The time will come when he will fall, like an overripe fruit grown in the gardens of our solitude.

There are tears which pierce through the earth and rise as stars in other skies. I wonder who has wept our stars?

What is the novelty of Christianity? It is like a thistle in the heart, pricking it at every dilation. Christianity delights in the sight of bloodstains, and its martyrs have transformed the world into a bloodbath. In this religion of blazing twilights, evil defeats the sublime.

Other religions have invented the happiness of slow dissolution; Christianity has made death a seed, and life its roots. Could there by any remedy against this germinating death, this *life* of death?

Francis of Assisi founded his order after hearing a voice saying to him during his prayer: "Go and rebuild my ruined house!" The Church owes a lot to such hallucinations! All the zealots of reformation were prompted by divine commands. It would be difficult to explain their courage or their madness otherwise. Not one would have done it alone! But no obstacle is unsurmountable when angelic voices cheer you along. It is our unhappy lot not to burn with inspiring fever. One does not hear voices in the cool breeze of calm thoughts, and angels speak only to musical ears.

Francis of Assisi's absolute perfection is unforgivable. He has no weaknesses that would render him more familiar, less remote. However, I think that I have found one humanizing excuse. When at the end of his life he was about to go blind, the doctors found the cause to be an excess of tears.

Saintliness is the overcoming of our condition as "creatures." The desire to be *in* God does not go with life *near* or *under* him, the lot of fallen creatures.

And if I cannot live, let me at least die in God. Or better still, let me be buried *alive* in him!

Whenever we exhaust all the possibilities of a musical theme, the void it leaves behind is infinite. Nothing can reveal divinity better than the inner multiplication, through memory, of a Bach fugue. After recollecting its feverish, ascending melody, we throw ourselves into God's arms. Music is the last emanation of the universe, just as God is music's final effluence.

I am like the sea which parts its waters to make room for God. Divine imperialism is man's reflux.

Oppressed by the solitude of matter, God has shed oceans of tears. Hence the sea's mysterious appeal, and our longing to drown in it, like a short cut to him through his tears.

He who has not shed tears on every seashore has not known the troubling vicinity of God, that solitude which forces upon us an even greater one.

I can only see my shadow in God. The closer I come to him, the longer it grows, and I run away chased by my own shadow.

Without God, all is night, and with him light is useless.

I despise Christians because they love men *at close quarters*. Only in the Sahara could I rediscover love.

✧

The fewer the solutions the livelier the thought!

✧

Since there really are no solutions, one is bound to turn round in a vicious circle. Thoughts fed on sadness and suffering take the form of aporias, symptoms of spiritual decline. The insoluble casts a shimmering shadow on the world, and lends it the incurable serious-ness of twilight. There are no solutions, only *cowardice* masquerading as such. All twilights are on my side.

✧

Mysticism revolves around the passion for ecstasy and a horror of the void. One cannot know one without the other. The road to ecstasy and the experience of the void presuppose a will to make the soul a *tabula rasa*, a striving towards psychological blankness. Once it has totally rejected the world, the soul is ripe for a long-term and fecund *emptiness*. Consciousness dilates beyond the limits of the cosmos. Stripping it of images is the essential condition for ecstatic spasms. One sees noth-ing except *nothingness*. And the latter has become *everything*. Ecstasy is plenitude in a void, a *full void*. It is an over-whelming frisson which convulses nothingness, an invasion of *being* in absolute emptiness. The void is the condition for ecstasy just as ecstasy is the condition for the void.

✧

Love of the absolute engenders a predilection for self-destruction. Hence the passion for monasteries and brothels. Cells and women, in both cases. Weariness

64

with life fares well in the shadow of whores and saintly women.

✧

The "appetite for God" of which St. John of the Cross speaks is first a negation of existence and only in the final instance its affirmation. For the man who with blighted hope has resigned himself to accepting the shadows of this world, such "appetite for God" can only be a symptom of nihilism. Its intensity proves to what extent one no longer belongs to this earth. One betrays a deficiency of vital instincts whenever one thinks instinctively about God. The fulcrum of divinity is at zero vitality.

✧

Mysticism is an eruption of the absolute into history. Like music, it is the crowning of culture, its ultimate justification.

✧

All nihilists have wrestled with God. One more proof of his kinship with nothingness. After you have trampled everything under foot, his is the last bastion of nothingness left.

✧

Men speak of God not only to "place" their madness somewhere, but also to dissimulate it. As long as you are busy with him you have an excuse for sadness and solitude. God? An official madness.

✧

Each time weariness with the world takes on a religious form, God appears like a sea of forgetfulness. Drowning in God is a refuge from our own individuality.

There are other times when we encounter him like a luminous zone at the end of a long regression inside ourselves. But the comfort we derive is smaller, for by finding him *in us,* we own him a little. We feel then that we have rights over him, for our acknowledgment does not surmount the limits of illusion.

The God-sea and the God-light alternate in our experience of divinity. In either case, forgetfulness is the end.

Listening to Bach, one sees God come into being. His music generates divinity.

After a Bach oratorio, cantata, or passion, one feels that God *must* be. Otherwise, Bach's music would be only heartrending illusion.

Theologians and philosophers wasted so many days and nights searching for proofs of his existence, ignoring the only valid one: Bach.

Sadness makes you God's prisoner.

Reason's only useful task: to comfort you for not being God. The more you think of God, the less you are. Thus God is nothing more than a projection of our longing for annihilation.

The idea of God is the most practical as well as the most dangerous of all ideas ever conceived. Through it, mankind is both saved and doomed.

The absolute is a presence soluble in blood.

In vain do we try to cast off the saints. They leave God behind them the way the bee leaves its sting.

Why do we recall the Greek cynics so rarely? They knew everything, and suffered the consequences of their supreme indiscretion. It took mankind another thousand years to gain back its naiveté. Compared to the cynics, Descartes, like Homer, seems a child. One is equally predestined to knowledge or to ignorance. Knowledge is like a melancholy sunset; ignorance, a dawn full of apprehensions.

It is better to forget the cynics. Their lack of timidity in front of knowledge betrays a dangerous lust for incurable diseases.

Good health is the best weapon against religion. Healthy bodies and healthy minds have never been shaken by religious fears. Christianity has exploited for its own benefit all the illnesses that plague mankind. Had Christ promised us *hygiene* instead of the heavenly kingdom, we would not have been seeking solace in saints ever since his death!

✧

How could Plotinus or Eckhart be so contemptuous of time, and never feel any regret for it? The failed mystic is the one who cannot cast off all temporal ties. Caught between mysticism and history, he wanders for ever in the no-man's-land connecting this world to the other. As with music and eroticism, the secret of successful mysticism is the defeat of time and individuation.

I can't help hearing a death knell ringing in eternity: therein lies my quarrel with mysticism.

Life in God is the death of being. One is not alone *with* him but *in* him. It is what St. John of the Cross mysteriously called "soledad en Dios." For him, the union of man's solitude with God's infinite desert is utter delight, a sign of their complete identity. What happens to the mystic during his divine adventure, *what does he do with God?* We do not know, for not even he can tell us.

If we had direct access to mystical joy without the trials which precede ecstasy, divine happiness would be available to everyone. But since there is no such availability, we are forced to climb a ladder without ever reaching its last step.

Next to the mystics' "soledad en Dios," there is another solitude, or rather an *exile* in him: the sensation of not feeling *at home* inside him.

To forget the saints, we must be bored with God. Once we are rid of God, who would dare bar our way? The angels and the saints, crushed under the ruins of his temple, cry out in pain.

It is easier for me to imagine the Alps turning into a weeping willow than to imagine a man who loves God. How such love comes about, God only knows. But not even God knows *why.* God is the burial ground of transcendental vagrants.

⬥

It is harder to forget saintly women, for they seduce us with their divine and melancholy beauty. God can easily disgust us once we've had enough of him. But we cling to the holy maidens whose tears we have avidly drunk, and whose sadness has been the source of unspeakable pleasures.

The last step towards nihilism is the disappearance into divinity.

The Greeks only *looked* at nature. Had they truly loved it, they would not have placed its mystery in transcendence. All religions are a dispossesion of nature.

Nothing but thorns bloom in God.

The mystics do not know anything about *loneliness in God.* They are blissfully ignorant of the tragedy which begins in God's proximity, the consciousness of insanity which torments those prostrate at his feet. Saints and mystics alike end in triumph when they penetrate divinity with erotic abandon. But their triumph proves nothing. We who pass *through* Divinity leave them behind, ignorant of the road which leads away from God. They have never asked themselves the question, "What begins *after* God," and for that I cannot forgive them.

The fall out of time is always preceded by a fainting fit, proof that physiology and eternity are closely related.

Life is a series of obsessions one must do away with. Aren't love, death, God, or saintliness interchangeable and circumstantial obsessions?

Askesis is one more proof that God is born out of a void of vitality. The more we die in the flesh and in time, the closer we are to him. God is a blight on all earthly joys.

The creation of man was a cosmic cataclysm, and its aftershocks have become God's nightmares. Man is a paradox of nature, equally removed from it and from God. The order of things in heaven and on earth has changed ever since the creation of consciousness. With it, God appeared in his true light as one more nothingness.

My definition of a musician: a man who hears through all his senses. Anna Magadalena, Bach's second wife, records in her diary the striking impression made by her husband's eyes: they were *listening* eyes.

She also recalls: "Once I went into his room while he was composing 'Ah, Golgotha!' from St. Matthew's Passion. I was amazed to see his face, usually calm and fresh pink, turned gray and covered with tears. He didn't even notice me, so I crept back outside, sat down on the step by his door and started to cry." Bach's music is the medium of heavenly transfiguration. In it there are no feelings, only God and the world, linked by a ladder of tears.

The saints weep. I comment on their tears. All we have left is commentary, since all the tears have already been wept.

Poets are interested in saints to the extent that they are either thought-provoking or comforting.

Without their madness, saints would merely be Christians.

For a man of genius, the absolute coincides with his private demons: for the saints, it is not only outside, but *beyond*. Though they act extravagantly, saints are more banal than the poets. Madness in the name of love and suffering is not very interesting. The poets have no ready-made excuses for their madness.

Baudelaire rivals St. John of the Cross. Rilke was a burgeoning saint. Poetic genius and saintliness share a secret penchant for self-destruction.

Memory becomes active once it ceases to operate in a temporal framework. The experience of eternity is *actuality*; it occurs anywhere and anyhow without reference to our past. It is but a leap out of time, so we do not need to remember anything. Whenever our essential past is concerned, i.e., the *eternity* which precedes time, only pretemporal memories can reveal it to us. There is a kind of memory, deep and dormant, which we rarely awaken. It goes all the way back to the beginning of time, to God and the limits of remembrance. It is *intelligible memory*.

All memories are symptoms of illness. Life in its pure state is absolute actuality. Memory is the negation of instinct, its hypertrophy, an incurable disease.

Eternity is not just another attribute of becoming, it is its negation. Human nature is equally divided between eternity and becoming. This division encompasses our tragedy.

Mankind has lived without God ever since it stripped him of his personal characteristics. By trying to widen the Almighty's sphere of influence, we have unwittingly put him beyond the pale. Whom shall we address if not a person who can listen and answer? Having gained so much space, he is everywhere and nowhere. Today he is at most the universal Absentee.

We have alienated God by magnifying him. Why have we denied him his heavenly modesty, what immeasurable pride has prompted us to falsify him? He has never been less than he is today, when he is everything! Thus we are punished for having been too generous with him. He who has lost God the person will never find him again, no matter how hard he searches for him in other guises.

By trying to help God, we exposed him to human jealousy. Thus, having tried to mend a cosmic error, we have destroyed the only priceless error.

Man's historical destiny is to experiment with the idea of God. Having exhausted all the possibilities of divine experience, he inevitably winds up loathing the absolute. Only then can he breathe freely. Yet the struggle against a God who has taken shelter in the innermost corners of our soul is fraught with ineffable misery, originating in the fear of losing him. It is as if one needs to devour God's last remains before reveling without hindrance in the freedom that follows upon annihilation.

The ambiguity of religion is born from a mixture of absurdity and finality. Religion is a smile masking cosmic nonsense, one last waft of perfume drifting over nothingness. Thus, when it runs out of arguments, religion finds recourse in tears. Only tears can still ensure universal equilibrium and keep God alive. Our longing for him will fade away with our last tear.

There are moments when one would like to lay down one's arms and dig one's grave close to God's; or maybe fall into the stony despair of an ascetic who discovers too late in life the futility of renunciation.

How tiresome is the idea of God! It is a fatal form of neurasthenia, its presence in consciousness causes fatigue, and a low, exhausting fever. How did so many saints manage to live to old age with their constant obsession with God? They even cut down on their sleep to have more time to think about him and worship him!

Artists can't be religious. To have faith one must remain passive vis-à-vis the world. The believer must not do anything. The artist can't believe because he has no time.

✧

In fact, there is only God and me. His silence invalidates us both.

✧

I can die in peace for I no longer expect anything from him. Our encounter has divided us even more. Each human life is one more proof of his nothingness.

How many people experience the fall from a height to a precipice? The parting from God has yet to be set to music.

Without God, everything is nothingness. But God is the supreme nothingness!

The final chapter of any metaphysics deals exclusively with God. Philosophical thought is always circling around God but rarely does it radiate from *inside* him. Philosophical thought is redeemed through human immanence in divinity. Once man has arrived *inside* God, he builds *over and above* him. Thus man surpasses himself; he would otherwise die under his own weight.

I am sorry sometimes that God no longer fills us with dread. If only we could feel again the primordial quiver of dread in front of the unknown!

The more we abandon ourselves to feelings, the more estranged from life we become. Paroxysms of feeling draw us out of ourselves into a realm bordering on the divine. Intense love, pain, or loathing reach their final limit in God. Without a transcendental theme, delirium is mere pathology. With divinity at its center, it becomes revelation, a crowning of the spirit. God and delirium shoulder each other. Ecstasy systematizes the experience of divinity. Delirium is an anticipation of ecstasy, whereas mystical delirium is complete ecstasy. God seems to take advantage of moments of delirium to remind some of us his presence.

✧

To be in harmony with the universe is to fall into wisdom. It means that you know everything, are in agreement with everything, but not with much else! All the sages put together are not worth a single one of Lear's curses or Ivan Karamazov's ravings. There is nothing blander or more comfortable than stoicism as both a practical and a theoretical justification of wisdom. Is there a greater spiritual vice than renunciation?

Disagreement is a sign of spiritual vitality. It culminates in disagreement with God. Were we to make peace with God, we wouldn't live anymore, he would live for us. As long as we assimilate ourselves to him we do not exist, whereas if we resist him, there is no reason for us to exist.

If I were tired of living, God would be my last resort. As long as I am still racked by despair, I can't leave off harrowing him.

I imagine man's isolation thus: a wintry landscape in which the snow is like materialized ingenuity; a light mist blurring the contours of the land; white silence, and in it, Man, ghost-like, an exile among the snow flakes.

God's destiny, like that of ordinary mortals in fact, is to be misunderstood. Yet there must be a few who understand him. If not, whence the painful certainty which grips us sometimes that we can no longer *progress* in him? And wherefore the long wakeful nights when we exhaust him through thought and remorse? How strange that we discover him so late, and that his absence leaves such a spiritual emptiness!

Only by thinking about him constantly and mercilessly, only by setting siege to his solitude can we win rich spoils in our battle with him. If we lose heart and go halfway only, he will be just one more failure.

The more one is obsessed with God, the less one is innocent. Nobody bothered about him in paradise. The fall brought about this divine torture. It's not possible to be conscious of divinity without guilt. Thus God is rarely to be found in an innocent soul.

Contact with divinity cancels innocence because every time one thinks of God one meddles with his affairs. "He who sees God will die!" The infernal expanses of divinity are as disturbing as vice. Those who have endowed God with virtues have only a superficial conception of him.

Theology is the negation of divinity. Looking for proofs of God's existence is a crazy idea. All the theological treatises put together are not worth a single sentence from Saint Teresa! We have not gained one certitude since the beginning of theology until today, for theology is the atheist's mode of believing. The most obscure mystical mumbo-jumbo is closer to God than the *Summa theologiae*, and a child's simple prayer offers a greater ontological guarantee than all ecumenical synods. All that is institution and theory ceases to be *life*. The church and theology have made possible God's endless agony. Only mysticism has given him life once in a while. Theology would be valuable were we to have a *theoretical* relation to God, which is easier than a *physiological* one. The poor maidservant who used to say that she only believed in God when she had a toothache puts all theologians to shame.

Were it not for our moments of inquisitive sadness, God would not exist.

We could replace theology with what a poet once called the "science of tears." It has *direct* arguments and an *immediate* method.

Nothing more exquisite or more disturbing than to have the thought of God occur while one lies in the arms of a whore! It is easy to think of him after a page from the Bible or after an oratorio, but God's presence manifested in the midst of vulgar debauchery has an infinitely greater impact: it brings loneliness and the dread of nothingness back to mind with full force.

I wish my heart were an organ pipe, and I the translator of God's silences.

I have always wondered about people who are "crazy about God," who have sacrificed everything for him, first of all their minds. Sometimes I surmise how one could die for him in a moment of morbid inspiration. Hence the immaterial attraction that death has for me. There is something rotten in the idea of God!

Few are the poets who know the genealogy of tears. For if they knew it, they would no longer say "I," but "God." We cry in God.

The obsession with God dislodges earthly love. One cannot love both God and a woman at the same time without being torn between them: they are incompatible with each other. One woman is enough to rid us of God, and God can rid us of all women.

Every revolt is directed against Creation. Any rebellious gesture, however small, undermines the universal order accepted by the slaves of God. One cannot be both for God and against his law. Yet out of love for him one could dismiss and despise Creation.

In his name one cannot rebel even against sin. For the supreme Reactionary, anarchy is the only sin.

Every revolt is atheistic. The plan of creation did not anticipate anarchy. We know very well that only *animals* lounged about in paradise. Then one of them got tired of it, gave up bliss, and became Man. Our whole history has been built on this first rebellion.

Someday this old shack we call the world will fall apart. How, we don't know, and we don't really care either. Since nothing has real substance, and life is a twirl in the void, its beginning and its end are meaningless.

Whenever I try to get closer to God, I'm hit by a wave of pity that surges towards his desolate heights. One would like to show sympathy toward this lonely, sad God of mourning. Pity for God is a human being's last solitude.

It may very well be that man's sole purpose is none other than to *think* of God. If we could either love him or ignore him, we would be saved. It is only by thinking of him that God makes one feel uncomfortable. Start prying into him and you are lost. Yet prying is man's very purpose. No wonder that God was done with in no time at all. He withstands many things, but thinking makes him lose substance. Yet there have been philosophers who have attributed to him infinite thought! God is nothing but an old frumpy coat which you must put on if you have nothing better to wear. What abject poverty!

Human history is in fact a divine drama. God is not only mixed up with it, he too suffers, but with infinitely more intensity, the process of creation and destruction which defines life. We have this unhappiness in common, but given his dimensions, it may consume him first. Our solidarity with him under the curse of existence is the reason why all irony directed towards him turns back against us. To doubt God is to be self-ironical. Who has suffered more than us mortals because he is not what he should have been?

Sometimes God is so easy to make out that just listening a bit more carefully to one's inner voice is enough. This is the explanation for the familiarity of those rare moments when revelation of the divine is experienced outside of ecstasy.

All forms of divinity are autobiographical. Not only do they come out of us, we are also *mirrored* in them. Divinity is introspection's double vision revealing the life of the soul as both *I* and *God.* We see ourselves in him and he sees himself in us.

Could God carry the weight of all my deficiencies? Wouldn't he succumb under the tremendous load of all my misfortunes?

I understand myself only through the image I have of him. Self-knowledge is only possible through him. He who does not think about God will forever remain a stranger to himself. God is self-knowledge, and universal history is a description of his various forms.

Thinking should be like musical meditation. Has any philosopher pursued a thought to its limits the way Bach or Beethoven develop and exhaust a musical theme? Even after having read the most profound thinkers, one still feels the need to begin anew. Only music gives definitive answers.

Thinking is not exhaustive; there are infinite variations on the theme of God. Thinking and poetry have intimidated him, but they have never solved the mystery gathered around his persona. Thus we have buried him with all his secrets. A mind-boggling adventure: first his, then ours as well.

Of all human beings, the hero is the one who thinks least about death. Yet is there anyone who has a greater unconscious longing for death? Thus paradox defines the hero's condition: he enjoys the voluptousness of death without awareness of it.

Spirit means renunciation. What would be the point of a second renunciation through heroism? Heroes abound at the dawn of civilizations, during pre-Homeric and Gothic epochs, when people, not having yet experienced spiritual torture, satisfy their thirst for renunciation through a derivative: heroism.

There is no link between the divine and the heroic. God has no heroic attributes. Jesus is a hero only to the extent that he is human.

Up to Beethoven, music was redolent of heaven. Beethoven's heroic tumult stripped divinity down to a human drama. I don't know of any music more *political* than his. It marks a triumph over the world but does not venture beyond it.

Titans are no longer attractive once we think of God. Intimations of God's supreme indifference render man's revolt utterly pointless. To be a hero only in the eyes of men is a paltry thing. There is no consolation in dying like a hero, i.e., misunderstood by the gods.

What would I do without Dutch landscape painting, without Salomon and Jacob Ruysdael or Aert van der Neer? Their landscapes awaken in me dreams animated by sea breezes, drifting clouds, and twilight colors. All of them are a commentary on melancholy. Trees and desolate patches of water under a sky too vast for their size; herds grazing not grass but infinity; men who don't seem to go anywhere, frozen in expectation under the shadows spreading over the land—it is a universe whose mystery is intensified by the very light itself. Vermeer van Delft, master of intimacy and confidential silences, showed us in his portraits and his interiors how to render silences palpable without abusing the technique of chiaroscuro. By contrast, Jacob Ruysdael, more of a poet than a painter, works with infinite spaces in which silences become palpable through a chiaroscuro of monumental proportions. In his paintings, you can almost *hear* the silence of twilight. Such is the wistful charm of Dutch landscape painting, to which is added the intimation of fraility without which melancholy would not be poetry.

Russia and Spain—two countries pregnant with God. Other countries know him, but do not carry him in their womb.

A nation's mission in this world is to reveal at least *one* of God's attributes, to show us one of his hidden aspects. By realizing in itself some of divinity's secret qualities, a nation diminishes the power of the Almighty, reduces his mystery.

Thousand of years of history have seriously jeopardized his authority. Nations have competed in worshiping him, ignorant of the evil they caused. Had all countries resembled Russia and Spain, he would be totally finished today. Russian and Spanish atheism is inspired by the Almighty: through atheism he defends himself against all-consuming faith. Our divine Father welcomes his sons, the atheists, with open arms!

Nobody has represented heavenly passion in painting better than El Greco. Has God ever been besieged by human figures with a greater and more intense aggression? Far from being the product of an optical deficiency, El Greco's oval faces represent the shape of human faces stretched towards God. To us, Spain is a flame; to God, it is a conflagration. The deserts of the earth and the sky are united through fire. Russia and Siberia are burning together with Spain and God.

The most skeptical Russian or Spaniard is more passionately in love with God than any German metaphysician. The chiaroscuro of Dutch painting cannot match in intensity the burning shadows of El Greco or Zurbaran's paintings. In spite of its deep mystery, Dutch chiaroscuro remains alienated and far removed from God. Melancholy is resistant to the absolute.

Between Spain and Holland lies the measureless distance from despair to melancholy. Even Rembrandt invites us to rest in his shadows, and his chiaroscuro is like a cradle in which we die peacefully, having lived without suffering. All of Rembrandt is nothing but the *expectation* of old age. It would be hard to find a more thoughtful and more resigned artist.

Among the Dutch, he alone understood God. (Could it be that for this reason he painted so few landscapes?) But his God does not de-form and dis-figure as in El Greco, he comes forth from mysterious shadows, steeped in profound but restrained piety. What a stroke of good luck that Rembrandt was a painter and not a philosopher! Wisdom has been Holland's curse, and it has taken it right out of history!

Is there another criterion for art besides closeness to heaven? Intensity and passion can be measured only in relation to the absolute. But this criterion gives us no solace. Both Russia and Spain teach us that we are never as close to God as to earn the right of being atheists!

All great ideas should be followed by an exclamation mark—a warning signal similar to the skull and cross-bones drawn on high-voltage transformers.

Could everything be so totally devoid of meaning? Each time I look up at the sky, I am unpleasantly reminded that there is no history.

Time is a consolation. But consciousness defeats time. There is no easy therapy against consciousness. Negating time is an illness. Purity and health in life are the apotheosis of futility. Eternity is rot, and God a carrion which the human worm feeds on.

There are many thinkers and dreamers who never feel the need for God. Sadness without the need for consolation does not guarantee a religious experience. Those limited to sadness per se are strangers to God. The absolute is a specific tonality of sadness.

Pascal established the difference between God and the *idea* of God when he distinguished between the God of Abraham and Job on the one hand and the philosophers' God on the other. One must add to his distinction the one between Bach and the rest of music, Teresa of Avila and the rest of the saints, Rilke and the rest of poetry.

The organ is a cosmogony of tears. It has a metaphysical resonance not to be found either in the cello or the flute, except, possibly, in their lyrical expression and their infinitely subtle nostalgic vibrations. But the absolute resonates directly through the organ. It is the least human instrument and it gives the impression that it plays itself. By contrast, the cello and the flute exhibit all the human flaws, transfigured by a supernatural regret.

You happen to walk into a church one day, you cast an indifferent glance at your surroundings, when suddenly the organ's powerful harmonics burst forth and overwhelm you; or, one melancholy afternoon, as you stroll aimlessly through the streets, the meditations of a cello or the sighs of a flute arrest your progress: could your solitude then be less than divine?

Forms and colors burn vertically in El Greco. In van Gogh's paintings too, objects are flames and colors burn, but horizontally, spreading out in space. Van Gogh is El Greco without God, without heaven.

An artist's center of gravity does not explain his formal structure and style so much as his inner atmosphere. For El Greco, the world throws itself towards God, while in van Gogh it collapses on its inner chaos.

Full of loathing for the world, we feel that we must rid ourselves of feelings. They are the cause of all our pointless commitments, prompting us to say a cowardly "yes!" to reality. Mad with fury, we fall into fits of secular saintliness, and compose our own epitaph. Thus we live our life as if it were a variation on the theme "Here lies. . . ."

✧

Prayer is the martyrdom of the spirit prompted by fear of solitude.

✧

Life is legalized, consecrated absurdity.

✧

The task of a solitary man is to be even more solitary.

✧

The dull sadness of monasteries wore an emptiness into the soul of the monks, known in the Middle Ages as *acedia.* Like nausea welling up from the desert of the heart, acedia is religious spleen. It is a loathing not *of* God but *in* him. Acedia gathers into itself the meaning of all those Sunday afternoons spent in the weighty silence of monasteries. It is Baudelaire's soul in the Middle Ages.

Ecstasy creates its own divine landscape; acedia disfigures the landscape, bleeds sap from nature, poisons life with an ennui which only we, accursed mortals, can still comprehend. Modern acedia is no longer monastic solitude—though our souls are our cloisters—but a void, and the dread of an inefficient, derelict God.

For the medieval monks God *was* even when he seemed dull, cruel, or absent. Our acedia has turned God into an ornament crowning all our doubts. For skeptics, the absolute has always been purely decorative.

✧

Tell me how you want to die, and I'll tell you who you are. In other words, how do you fill out an empty life? With women, books, or wordly ambitions? No matter what you do, the starting point is boredom, and the end self-destruction. The emblem of our fate: the sky teeming with worms. Baudelaire taught me that life is the ecstasy of worms in the sun, and happiness the dance of worms.

✧

Have you looked at yourself in the mirror when nothing stood between you and death? Have you questioned your eyes? And by looking into them, have you then understood that you cannot die? Your pupils dilated by conquered terror are more impenetrable than the Sphinx. From their glassy immobility a certitude, strangely tonic in its brief mysterious form, is born: *you cannot die.* It comes from the silence of our gaze meeting itself, the Egyptian calmness of a dream facing the terror of death. Each time the fear of death grabs you, look in the mirror. You will then understand why you can never die. Your eyes know everything. For in them there are specks of nothingness, which assure you that nothing more can happen.

✧

The decadence of a nation coincides with its maximum of collective lucidity. History makes instincts grow weaker, and on their ruin boredom blossoms. The English are a nation of pirates who got bored once they had robbed the world. The Romans were not wiped out by the invasions of the barbarians, nor by the Christian virus, but by a more subtle evil, boredom. Once they began to have unlimited free time, they did not know how to employ it. Free time is a bearable curse for a thinker, but for a people it is pure torture. What does free time mean, if not duration without content?

Dawn is full of ideals, twilight only of ideas. Passion is replaced by the need for diversion. Epicureanism and

Stoicism were the cures that ancient Greece, in the throes of its final agony, tried to apply to its *mal du siècle*. These, like the multiple religions of Alexandrian syncretism were mere palliatives which masked the illness without annulling its virulence. A satiated people suffers from spleen as much as a man who has lived too long and knows too much.

The difference between the sweaty, earthy boredom of the Russians and the perfumed refinements of French and English boredom is smaller than it seems. They are both caused by a deficiency of the blood. An organic antinomy causes boredom to secrete corrosive toxins of anxiety. Any kind of boredom will reveal two things to us: our body and the nothingness of the world.

The only way to love God is to hate him. Not even infallible proof of his nonexistence could suppress the fury of Man, who has invented God to quench his thirst for love and, especially, hate. Is he anything but the fateful moment when our life totters on the brink of destruction? Who cares whether he is or not since through him lucidity balances itself out with madness and we discharge our fury by embracing him with murderous passion?

Boredom is the simplest way to abolish time, ecstasy the most complex. The more bored one is, the more self-conscious. Illnesses affect specific places in the body, which can be isolated and cured. But boredom spreads over the entire body like a cancer, seeps into our organs and carves out holes that resemble a system of underground caves. Life is our solution to boredom. Melancholy, sadness, despair, terror, and ecstasy grow out of boredom's thick trunk. There are flowers of melancholy and of sadness, but only boredom has roots.

The secret is to know how to be bored in an *essential* way. Most people, however, never even scratch the surface of boredom. To live *real* boredom, one must have *style*.

The soul of those haunted by God is like a decayed spring, littered with half-withered flowers and rotten buds, swept by foul odors. It is the soul of blackmailing saints such as Léon Bloy, and of anti-Christian Christians such as Nietzsche. I regret that I am not Judas to betray God and know remorse.

The urge to desecrate tombs and to give life to cemeteries in an apocalypse of springtime! There is life only in spiting death's absoluteness. Simple peasants knew it when they made love in cemeteries and challenged death's aggressiveness with their passionate sighs. Sexuality transfigured by tombstones, how tantalizing!

It is impossible for us to anticipate the exact moment when we shall have intimations of the Last Judgment. Sometimes, in the middle of a vulgar fit of anger, or while delivering ourselves of a weighty banality, a sort of terminal emotion seizes us. We can then talk for hours on end with people we despise, we can say happy and irrelevant things without their noticing how close we are to the Last Judgment, and how lost to the world! He who does not have a constant expectation of the End is too cowardly to respond to this last provocation from God by having an all-out fight with the master of universal stupidity, the maker of a mediocre and superfluous world.

One does not need to be a Christian in order to fear the Last Judgment, or even to understand it. Christianity did nothing but exploit human anguish to make top profits for an unscrupulous divinity whose best ally was dread.

The Last Judgment appears in consciousness as a vague and unpredictable moment. It is nevertheless a *stage* of anxiety. You think that you are moving with spiteful dread through absolute infinity, when suddenly there is a new obstacle: the Last Judgment. So what! Is God trying to kill us once more?

Boredom is the only argument against immortality. From it derive all our negations.

I'm looking for what *is.* A pointless search. Let's march to the Last Judgment with flowers in our buttonholes!

I listen to silence and I cannot stifle its voice: *it's all over.* These words heralded the beginning of the world, since only silence preceded it.

Compared to the Last Judgment, everything seems frivolous, even the idea of God. Once there, you are ashamed of all that does not belong to the *end.*

✧

With springtime comes a longing for death. The Last Judgment is the religious expression of this longing.

✧

The Last Judgment is God's meeting with the future, i.e., with the graves.

✧

Though the Last Judgment is mere nonsense and an insult to our intelligence, it nevertheless constitutes an useful concept that explains our nothingness. The representation of the end of history, whether in sacred or profane form, is essential to our spirit. Thus the most absurd idea acquires the force of destiny.

✧

Irony is an exercise in metaphysical frivolity. The ironic "I" annihilates the world. When nothing is left standing, one experiences exciting power thrills. The ironic mode is a ruse of self-importance: to make up for its nonexistence, the "I" becomes everything. Irony becomes serious when it yields an implacable vision of nothingness. Tragedy is the last stage of irony.

✧

All stands still, even God. Only our heartbeats remind us that once there was Time. He who does not know that he has a heart does not know that Time exists and that he lives in Time. The beating of our heart threw us out of paradise; when we understood its meaning we fell into Time.

✧

The repression of criminal impulses is a major cause of unhappiness. How many frustrations and how many individuals we could get rid of if we were to let ourselves go! We bury in our souls the corpses of those we have not killed. Misanthropy is the miasma of their putrefying carcasses. There is a failed executioner in each of us.

The world is divided between owners and beggars. Stuck in the middle, the poor form the colorless content of history. Owners and beggars alike are reactionaries. Neither wish for change or progress. The poor are left to struggle. Without them society would be a meaningless concept: their hopes are society's arteries, and their despair the blood of history. The owners and the beggars are parasites on the eternal poor. There are many recipes against wretchedness, but none against poverty.

The passion for the absolute in the soul of a skeptic is like an angel grafted on a leper. Everything that is neither God nor worm is a hybrid. Since we cannot be guardians of infinity, there is nothing left for us to do except mind the corpses!

There will be no cure for melancholy as long as there is spring. Nature itself is taken ill in springtime, this sensual and cruel season which makes you want to love and die.

Venice is not a historic reality but a function of melancholy, a town of tears caught between doubts and dreams.

I often think of a hermeneutics of tears, which would uncover their origins and list all possible interpretations. What would we gain by it? We would then know all the high points of history, and do without "events," since we would know how many times in the course of history Man rose above himself. Tears bestow on becoming an aura of eternity; they save it. Thus, for example, what would war be without them? Tears transfigure crime and justify it. They hold the key to the secrets of the universe. A hermeneutics of tears would show us the way that leads from ecstasy to anathema.

There are times when you want to go on a hunger strike—you long to be abandoned and humiliated, spat upon by passersby, dragged in the gutter, giving up the ghost among whores and beggars. But your fellow creatures are so cruel that they deny you the freedom to die of hunger. Prompted by an indiscreet pity, they moisten your lips just in time to rob you of your liberation. Society takes everything away from you but it prevents you from dying. And thus you begin to fear that you will miss every good opportunity to croak!

The frightful suspicion that God might be a second-rank problem tears me away from life. Inspired by a lucidity close to madness, such suspicions make me cross my arms and shrug my shoulders: what else can I do?

Could it be that even God has been corrupted by the futility of existence? Could the illness of the inessential have affected his essence? It must be so, since we doubt both his health and his virtue! God is no longer; not even our curses could bring him back to us. In what old people's home does he drag on his existence? I understand now: he is the absolute that *spares* itself! This world does not deserve anything better than a senile God.

Life is a reality only for wholesome people, high priests of eternal stupidity!

The ringing of bells announces the Last Judgment. For two thousand years bells have been predicting the end, filling with solemnity the agony to which Christianity has condemned us. When their ringing echoes inside you, you are ripe for the Judgment, and if your heart sounds like a broken bell, it means that the sentence is without appeal.

Mysticism is without meaning as long as you don't hear the music of silence.

There are moments when even the most humble Christian converses with God on an equal basis. Religion allows our pride these small satisfactions without which we would die suffocated by too much modesty. Atheism flatters our love of liberty: addressing God *from above* raises pride to the status of semidivinity. He who has never had contempt for God is predestined to slavery. We are *us* only to the extent that we humiliate him.

He who is not happy *naturally* knows only the happiness that follows after moments of despair. I'm afraid of falling prey to an insufferable happiness which, by avenging my past full of dread, would also avenge the misfortune of my having been born.

From a Christian point of view, the leper who loves his leprosy is superior to the one who merely accepts it, the dying man who suffers to the one who has resigned himself, despair to compromise. By legitimizing fever, Christianity has made possible a "culture" of saints.

Without illness there is no absolute knowledge. Illness is the primary cause of history; sin, only a secondary one.

Consciousness is a symptom of estrangement from life caused by illness. Everything that is *not* nature was revealed to the first sick man when he looked up at the sky for the first time.

I am fond of nations of astronomers such as the Chaldeans, Assyrians, Egyptians, pre-Columbians. They refused to make history out of love for the sky. A nation that loves neither the sky nor earthly conquests should not be allowed to live. There are only two ways to die right: on the battlefield or under the gaze of a star.

We are *not* when we are at one with the world. Our desire to escape the world and thus be ourselves sends us on a quest for suffering. Asceticism is the paroxysm of such desire, a systematic insomnia and starvation. Self-torture intensifies subjectivity. Suso's torments, for example, so minutely detailed in their horror, aim at constant wakefulness and bloody lucidity, as if the mystic feared that God would desert him during a lull in his agony. Once you have tasted the joys of suffering, you are hooked on them for ever. As Margaret Mary Alacoque used to say, "life is unbearable without suffering!" Through pain, we have hoisted ourselves to God's level.

All conversions are sudden but they take years germinating underground. We take the road to conversion at the first disappointment in life. Divine revelations break out after a long period of incubation; God, like pus, grows slowly to a head. We have a conversion if the divine boil bursts; if not, we live for the rest of our days with poison in our veins, i.e., with a God who refuses to show himself.

"The Age of Innocence." The more one looks at Reynolds' painting the more one realizes that our greatest failure is to have ceased to be children. Paradise is a projection in the past of this early stage in our life, our only comfort for having lost our childhood. Look closely at the child's delicate hand held timidly against his breast as if to protect his happiness. Has Reynolds understood all this? Or could it be that those large, shadowy eyes express a vague fear of losses to come? Children, like lovers, can foretell the end of happiness.

I have always loved tears, innocence, and nihilism; those who know everything as well as the blissfully ignorant; failures and children.

Adolescence is an intermediary stage linking the paradise of childhood to the inferno of failure.

Failure thrusts us into a paroxysm of lucidity. The world becomes transparent in the implacable eye of the sterile and clear-sighted man who no longer believes in anything. The failed man knows everything even though he may be illiterate. Dismissive of everything, he is a La Rochefoucauld without genius.

"Solitude has made me contemporary with the dead" (Barrès). There is no life, only eternity, in solitude.

A dull Sunday afternoon in the spring, its dead silence suddenly split by the crow of a rooster in which there are intimations of the Last Judgment.

Were I a poet I wouldn't allow Nero to go unavenged. I know something about the melancholy of mad emperors. Without the likes of Nero, the deaths of empires lack style, decadence is uninteresting.

Raskolnikov was unquestionably right: on the one hand there is the crowd living like automata according to the laws of nature; and on the other, the elected few to whom all is permitted since they atone for the shame of life's mediocrity through the tragic intensity of their own lives. But then why does Raskolnikov fail? Why is he eaten by remorse after the crime? Could it be that Dostoevsky feared the consequences of his own principles? But a man who faced death no longer thinks of consequences. Raskolnikov's failure is Dostoevsky's own cowardice.

A criminal saint represents the height of ambivalence, a thought worthy of Shakespeare and Dostoevsky.

Religion exploits latent madness for the good of the community. Churches are undercover hospices. They harness excessive enthusiasms, legalize doses of transcendental poison, and thus prevent the world from turning into a madhouse.

There is so much knowledge in melancholy that we could call it a vice.

It is a well-known fact that saints weep when they remember a divine revelation. Ignatius of Loyola, for example, had the revelation of the Holy Trinity during a religious procession, and would start to weep abundantly every time he recalled that moment. The crowd does not know the *then*, that moment of otherwordly happiness on which one's whole life turns. Saints have a different conception of history: their only historic event is revelation, which, however, annuls history.

According to the mystics, God alone can say "I." Here I am, God, awaiting the Last Judgment along with everybody else. You will then judge us *en masse*, for you don't dare look our loneliness in the face.

One melancholy cures another.

I won't die before I have killed everything in myself. I want to stifle the lamentations of space, crush the cosmic organ! No dying sun will find its reflection in my frozen tears.

Weary of consciousness, one dives into the ocean of the soul, and swims among fantastic shapes of aquatic vegetation, mere reflections of the world outside.

✧

The heart in mourning prompts us to think.

✧

I hear the bones cracking in their coffins, a sound heralding the Last Judgment. But we, the living, have already had our reckoning with God!

✧

It would be hard to find a more self-denying mystic than Eckhart, who totally managed to repress his animal instincts. His rejection of nature led to his *Abgeschiedenheit*, or detachment from wordly things, a precondition for attachment to God. Aware of the painful dissonance between life and eternity, he gave up the former without the least hesitation.

✧

Wherefore the need to add to Ecclesiastes when everything is already in it? Even more than that, whatever is not in it, is false. "Then my heart was moved to despair." Or rather, to truth.

"For too much wisdom increases the bitterness of our lot, and he who knows too much multiplies his suffering."

Ecclesiastes is a challenging revelation of truths which life, forever the accomplice of futility, battles against furiously.

✧

Good health lacks drama. After a long illness, our cured body imprisons us in poisoned, carnal boredom.

Each pain leaves behind an emptiness that can never be filled again. When you become prey to an incurable boredom, illness seems a welcome distraction.

Boredom is melancholic stillness, while despair is boredom burning at the stake. They are both born out of disgust with life.

There are no conversions. St. Paul had always already believed. Determinism forces us to expiate the whims of existence. Man believes, erroneously, that he lives as the wind blows. He has forgotten the winds of fatality!

An anxiety born out of nothing suddenly grows in us and confirms our homelessness. It is not "psychological" anxiety, it has something to do with what we call our soul. In it is reflected the torment of individuation, the ancient struggle between chaos and form. I can never forget those moments when matter defied God.

Disjunction from life develops a taste for geometry. We begin to see the world in fixed forms, frozen lines, rigid contours. Once the joy of Becoming is gone, everything perishes through too much symmetry. What is known as the "geometrism" of so many kinds of madness may very well be an exacerbation of the disposition towards immobility characteristic of depressions. Love of forms betrays a partiality for death. The sadder we are, the more things stand still, until everything is frozen stiff.

"Suffering is the cause of consciousness" (Dostoevsky). Men belong to two categories: those who have understood this, and the others.

✧

Time is the framework for seeking solutions; death is *the* solution.

✧

No matter how educated you are, if you don't think intensely about death, you are a mere fool. A great scholar—if he is nothing but that—is inferior to an illiterate peasant haunted by final questions. Generally speaking, science has dulled people's minds by diminishing their metaphysical consciousness.

✧

As you roam through the streets of a town, the world seems to be still in its place. But look out the window and all will vanish. How can a mere piece of transparent glass separate us from life to such an extent? In fact windows bar us from the world more than prison walls. By looking at life one begins to forget it.

✧

A time will come when worms will dream, nestled in my bones—a dreadful thought since it is akin to a memory.

✧

Schopenhauer maintains that, if we were to invite the dead back to life, they would refuse. I believe, on the contrary, that they would die a second time from too much joy.

✧

The more I read the pessimists, the more I love life. After reading Schopenhauer, I always feel like a bridegroom on his wedding night. Schopenhauer is right to maintain that life is a dream. But he is wrong to condemn illusions instead of cultivating them, for he thereby implies that there might be something better beyond them.

Only ecstasy cures us of pessimism.

Life would be unbearable if it were real. As a dream, it is a mixture of charm and terror to which we gladly abandon ourselves.

Consciousness is nature's nightmare.

Sunlight is not a good topic for poetry. You can be grateful for the sun, but can you sing its praises? The Egyptians made the sun a god so that they could compose hymns in its honor. Light is indiscreet, and when you are unhappy it is downright vexing. The sun describes a curve of happiness, but plenitude has never been a source of poetry.

The course of meditation: you begin by ignoring the object and end by ignoring the world.

All landscapes, and nature in general, are a desertion from temporality. Hence the curious feeling that nothing ever really is, every time we abandon ourselves to this dream of matter called nature.

Man has played hooky from nature. His successful evasion is his tragedy.

Love of nature is an expression of regret. One loves it least when one has no consciousness. When one is part of a landscape, one cannot appreciate it. The dim-witted and the blessed are not descended from Adam.

Nietzsche says somewhere: "You have been searching for the heaviest load, and you have found yourself!"

The awareness of time prompts men into action. Whoever lives in time must become its victim, for time would belie its own nature if it did not swallow up everything. The roots of our will to self-destruct lie in our desire to compete with time.

The company of mortals is, for a lucid man, pure torture. You have not understood our human tragedy if you have not bled to death, having lived among your peers in full consciousness.

You are free only to the extent that you execrate humanity. One must hate it to have the freedom to embrace so many useless perfections, the sadness and the bliss that lie beyond history, out of time. Any commitment to the cause of humanity betrays lack of taste and distinction. Hatred of man makes you love nature as a way to renunciation and freedom rather than, in the romantic fashion, as a stage in a spiritual odyssey. Having debased ourselves by dabbling in Becoming, it is high time we rediscovered our initial identity, which consciousness has shattered in a delirium of megalomania. I can't see a landscape without longing to destroy everything that is noncosmic in me. Overwhelmed by vegetable nostalgia and earthly regrets, I would like to become plant and die at sunset every day.

Life resembles springtime hysteria.

I am neither unhappy enough to be a poet nor as indifferent as a philosopher. But I am lucid enough to be a condemned man.

"I live on what makes other people die" (Michelangelo). There is no better definition of loneliness.

The world is nothing but a place in which we exercise our sadness. We need something to think about, and so we have made it into an object for meditation. Consequently, thought never misses an opportunity to destroy it.

After ecstatic joy comes the plunge into the deep sea of triviality.
The earth has grown musty from too many tears.

Boredom is tuneless matter.
Melancholy is the unconscious music of the soul.
Tears are music in material form.

Buddha must have been an optimist. Otherwise wouldn't he have noticed that pain defines not only everything there is but also what is not? Being and nothingness *exist* only through suffering. What is the void if not a dream of pain that has not come true? Nirvana represents ethereal suffering, a more refined form of torture. Absence signifies lack of being but not of pain. For pain precedes everything, even God.

I don't think that I have missed any opportunity for being sad. It is my human vocation.

I have never felt closer to death than in the moments when I loved live most. Terror ties me to the world more than voluptuous plenitude.

If I didn't drag death after me through the ups and downs of life, I would seek a place among animals to slumber like them in unconscious torpor. Am I attached to death only by a secret vegetable longing, a sort of complicity with Nature's funereal movements? Or rather, is it pride, a refusal to ignore the fact that we are bound to die? For nothing is more flattering than the thought of death—only *the thought,* though, not death it-self.

As long as I live I shall not allow myself to forget that I shall die; I am waiting for death so that I can forget about it.

The hatred of everything, of beings as well as of things, generates images of desolation. We begin to re-gret that there are too few deserts on this earth, we want to flatten the mountains, we dream of harsh Mongolian sunsets.

Christian ascetics thought that only the desert was without sin, and compared it to angels. In other words, there is purity only where nothing grows.

While reading subtle and useless philosophical po-lemics at the library, an irresistible longing for the desolation of deserts would sometimes grab hold of me. Then I would begin to see everything topsy-turvy, and revel in the absurdity of logical problems. It was as if rocks started to tumble down, dislocating concepts in a massive landslide of the spirit.

✧

The approach of death revives the sexual instinct: youthful desires burn again in a sickly conflagration of the blood. Death and sexuality mingle together in the spasms of agony and render it both terrifying and voluptuous. Were someone who knows nothing about sexual intercourse to overhear two people making love, he would think he is witnessing a deathbed scene, so closely does death resemble life at its supreme moment. One can't deny the funereal nature of sexuality: the same temporary hoarseness in the voice, the same complicity with the shadows, the same strange and disgusting bestiality casting a dismall pall on the pleasures of a delicate soul. When the will to die is intense, it becomes stimulating, serving life more than any human hope, stirring up our pride more than any passion.

✧

The desire to humiliate oneself out of spite for humanity, to play the victim, the monster, the beast! The more one wants to collaborate, the more one thinks altruistically about the other, the more inferior one is. *The other does not exist*—this is an obvious and comforting conclusion. To be alone, horribly alone, is the only imperative, and it must be obeyed at any price. The universe is a solitary space, and all its creatures do nothing but reinforce its solitude. In it, I have never met anyone, I have only stumbled across ghosts.

✧

Silence can be so deep sometimes that you hear thoughts rustling in freshly dug graves. The light flutter of butterfly wings in the mountains, when the wailing of the wind dies down, vexes even their hushed silence. It is at such moments that you notice the distant pale blue sky, and fall in love with its seraphic and silent stupidity. I love the sky because it is not intelligent. I suspect the stars have never known a thing.

Would we remember anything that was not tinged with bitterness and replete with intimations of mortality? Without the promise of suffering a woman brings with her when she thinks she makes us happy, love would be powerless to attenuate the dullness of life. The trace of pleasure in the soul? A crater of lucidity.

I often think of those anarchists who, before the crime, shut themselves up with women to drown in orgy the last shreds of commitment and remorse. Suicide, crime, exile, all choices that favor solitude, are inextricably bound up with images of women, for breaking with women symbolizes the renunciation of life. Misogynists, philosophers, and slaves have reduced women either to the constructive role of motherhood or to futile whoredom—out of hatred, wisdom, or stupidity respectively. But because women witness their self-destructive moments, because men need them in their dark agony, I feel less contempt for these creatures who, faced with the choice between sainthood and harlotry, suffer a drama of which we remain utterly ignorant.

The highest homage you can pay a woman is to think

of her when you have nothing more to lose. If women were not so central to our renunciations, we would have a right to despise and pity them. But death lends them a helping hand.

Our cosmic terror springs from the memory of the endless night against which God fought his first battle. He partly won, for he made night and day alternate. Man tried to establish the reign of day by conquering the night altogether; he was successful only in his imagination. We sleep not to rest but to forget the night we should have defeated.

From the cradle to the grave, each individual pays for the sin of not being God. That's why life is an uninterrupted religious crisis, superficial for believers, shattering for doubters.

We live in the shadow of our disappointments and wounded self-esteem. Our mad thirst for power cannot be quenched by anything in this world. This earth is not big enough for the devastating sweep of our godlike drives.

Religion comforts us for the defeat of our will to power. It adds new worlds to ours, and thus brings us hope of new conquests and new victories. We are converted to religion out of fear of suffocating within the narrow confines of this world. Thus a mystical soul knows no other enemy but God. He is one last stronghold that must be conquered.

I think of Man and see only shadows; I think of shadows and see only myself.

✧

We take turns sharing power with God. Hence two irreconcilable ways of looking at the world, since neither we nor God will make concessions.

I sometimes feel that those philosophers who explained the relationship between body and soul by seeing divine intervention in every action must have been right, though only partially. They did not sense that this world would have returned to chaos without God's constant intervention at every moment. Everything must be in agreement; divine goodwill contributes to this precarious equilibrium.

God is meddlesome, he is present everywhere. Could we smile without his approval? The faithful who invoke him at every turn know very well that the world left to its own devices would self-destruct. What would happen, I wonder, if God would return to his original passivity?

One cannot share power with God. One can replace him, follow after him, but one can never stand next to him, for he hates Man's pride. Man either loses himself in God or taunts him, but no one has ever remained level-headed in his presence. To be God's temporary replacement is Man's unique ambition.

Our failures are nowhere more in evidence than in the mysterious swinging motion that throws us far from God and brings us back to him. An alternation of triumphs and failures, it inscribes the entire hopelessness of our destiny.

I often think of the hermits of ancient Egypt who dug their own graves and wept in them day and night. When asked why they cried they replied that they wept for their soul.

In the infinity of the desert, a grave is an oasis, a place for comfort. To have a fixed point in space, one digs a hole in the desert. And one dies so that one won't get lost.

❖

Why do you ransack my memory? What's the use of remembering me? Will you ever be able to measure your fall and the presence of my anxiety within your own?

Turn your back on creation, and save me by forgetting me!

Forget me, for I want to be free, and never fear, I shall not waste my thoughts on you! Dead to each other, who would prevent us from doing as we pleased in this deserted cemetery to which, in your divine ignorance, you have given the name Life!

❖

It has often been said that as long as there is suffering there will also be a God. But nobody seems to have noticed that suffering can also negate God, and once voided by excessive suffering, nothing in the world can restore him to power. Negating God in the name of rationalism, skepticism, or indifference pales in comparison with the rejection of God sprung from the frenzy of agony.

The ultimate goal of all religions: life as a diminution of the soul.

I no longer have anything to share with anyone. Except with God, for just a while longer.

The more shocking a paradox about God is, the better it expresses his essence. Curses are closer to God than theology and philosophical meditation. Aimed at men, they are vulgar and of no consequence. One swears at a man's God, not at the man. The latter is innocent; God is the source of error and sin. Adam's fall was a divine calamity in the first place. God realized in Man all his possibilities for imperfection and corruption. We were made to save divine perfection. All that was "existence" in God, temporal infection and decay, was rerouted through men, while God salvaged his nothingness. We are his dump into which he has emptied himself.

Since we carry God's burden, we feel entitled to swear at him. God suspects this, and if he has sent Jesus to relieve us of our pain, he has done so out of remorse, not pity.

In the last stage of sadness, there are no longer any differences between tears and stones. The heart turns into rock, and the devils skate on your frozen blood.

All that is Life in me urges me to give up God.

One starts to believe in God out of pride, which is an honorable, if not an altogether pleasant, act. If you don't take an interest in him, you end up interested in mankind. Could you fall any lower than that?

⬥

The dead center of existence: when it is all the same to you whether you read a newspaper article or think of God.

⬥

Man cannot decide between freedom and happiness. On one side, infinity and pain; on the other, security and mediocrity. Man is too proud to accept happiness, and has fallen too low to have contempt for it.

Happiness engenders inferiority complexes. Who can be proud because he does not suffer? The awkwardness of ordinary people in front of those who suffer betrays our conviction that pain is distinctive and confers originality upon a human being. For one does not become a man through science, art or religion—to say nothing of philosophy—but through a self-conscious rejection of happiness, through a fundamental inability to be happy.

⬥

The moralists were naive enough to distinguish despair from pride. We seem to oscillate between hopelessness and pride; in fact we are too proud to hope. The less hope we have, the more proud we are. Despair and pride grow so closely together that even the keenest observer cannot tell them apart. Pride forbids hope, and prevents us from escaping the abyss of the self. Despair takes on a somber air of grandeur without which pride would be a mere petty game or a pitiful illusion.

⬥

As a function of despair, God should continue to exist even in the face of irrefutable proof that he does not exist. Truly, everything can be used as argument for or against him, because everything in the world both confirms and denies his divinity. Blasphemy and prayer are equally justified. When uttered in the same breath, one comes very close to the Supreme Equivocator.

✧

Every time I am sad it is as if each fiber in my body had started to think, as if poison had seeped into each cell, and depression enveloped me like a shroud. Sickness is the crisis of organic reflexivity. Tissues begin to be aware of themselves, individual organs acquire consciousness and separate from the rest of the body. Only in sickness do we realize how little we are in control of ourselves. Illness makes our body parts independent, while we remain their slave until the end. Illness is an organic state of consciousness, the spirit lost in the body.

✧

The restlessness of sleepless nights digs trenches where the corpses of memory are rotting.

✧

When everything is rot, and bones and faiths alike begin to rattle, a sudden light erupts and lifts your spirits. Is it the phosphorescent light of rot? Who could tell? No terror can be compared to this instant of paradise in which you forgive God and forget yourself!

✧

Life must have poured its last dregs in me, for nothing else could explain my dread of drowning in deep and stagnant waters. I am like those fish who die stranded in swamps, away from their usual habitat.

Man—a hero of semidarkness—swims in dead waters and stirs them only to be sure that they will not fail to swallow him.

Every time I look for a word that will fill me with sad contentment, I invariably come across the same one: forgetfulness. Not to remember anything, to look but not to see, to sleep with eyes open towards the Incomprehensible!

Such fierce longing to press God on my heart as if he were a loved one in the throes of agony, to beg of him one last proof of his love only to find myself with his corpse in my arms!

In *King Lear*, Shakespeare defines madness as a separation of the spirit from disgust of life.

This is the madmen's good fortune. Their spirit works *next* to sadness, which remains a world apart. We are left with the difficult task of finding a balance between weariness and the spirit. Madmen hardly ever come face to face with their own sadness. Lucidity is a misfortune.

How pleasant to have always handy a German mystic, a Hindu poet, or a French moralist for use in our daily exile!

Read day and night, devour books—these sleeping pills—not to know but to forget! Through books you can retrace your way back to the origins of spleen, discarding history and its illusions.

The regret of not being plants brings us closer to paradise than any religion. One *is* in paradise only as a plant. But we left that stage a long time ago: we would have to destroy so much to recover paradise! Sin is the impossibility of forgetfulness. The fall—emblem of our human condition—is a nervous exacerbation of consciousness. Thus a human being can only be *next* to God, whereas plants sleep *in* him the sleep of eternal forgetfulness. The more awake we are, the greater the nostalgia that sends us in quest of paradise, the sharper the pangs of remorse that reunite us with the vegetable world.

I could easily convert to a religion which preaches that to die is shameful. Christianity has flattered too much the most intimate part of ourselves, turning death into a triumph of virtue. Agony is Christianity's normal climate. Everybody dies in this religion, even God, as if there were not enough corpses already and time weren't the slaughterhouse of the universe!

It's neither easy nor pleasant to fight with God constantly. But once you start, prompted by an indefinite urge, you lose all sense of restraint. *Superbia* is the name for Man's presumption. It is the ego's delirium of megalomania, Man's tragic fate. Without this source of all of our follies and pettinesses, history would be inconceivable. Its ultimate form of expression is constant usurpation of God by Man. He who has experienced it to the last degree in his solitude can have only one rival: God.

If you believe in God, you are mad without having gone mad. It is similar to being sick without suffering from any specific illness.

All that adheres to this world is trivial. That's why there are no inferior religions. Even the most primitive sacred frisson lends a soul to appearances. *In* the world, grace turns to ashes; *beyond,* even nothingness becomes grace.

Had we thought about it a little, we could have made God happy. But now we have abandoned him, and he is lonelier than at the beginning of the world.

According to Eckhart, God hates nothing more than time and our commitment to it. In their longing for eternity, God and Eckhart have only contempt for "the smell and taste of time."

Self-conscious rejection of the absolute is the best way to resist God; thus illusion, the substance of life, is saved.

Children scare me. Their eyes contain too many promises of unhappiness. Why do they want to grow up? Children, like madmen, are graced with innate genius, soon lost in the void of lucidity.

Life is a state of inebriation crossed by sudden flashes of doubt. Most normal individuals are dead drunk. One wouldn't even dare breathe if one were sober.

As long as music addressed God and not men—as it has done since Beethoven—it was the opium dream of mortals. Once upon a time, it told of God's loneliness, and consequently of ours. The violins were the sighs of archangels, the flute the angels' lamentations, the organ the saints' imprecations. Bach, and the Italian masters of the same period, did not express feelings, they served heaven. It was easy then to suspend your humanity and abandon yourself in God.

Can I ever forgive this earth for counting me among its own, but only as an intruder?

"One thought of God is worth more than the entire world" (Catherine Emmerich). Poor saint, she was so terribly right!

Life is not, and death is a dream. Suffering has invented them both as self-justification. Man alone is torn between an unreality and an illusion.

Life is too full of death for death to add anything to it.

In the depths of our consciousness, paradise moans and memories weep. In this lamentation, we descry the metaphysical meaning of tears, and perceive life's unfolding as regret.

Once you have thought a lot about death, you start to wonder if it wasn't all a huge lie. Having risen *above* death, the truths below appear as illusions.

I am altogether too much of a Christian. I can tell from the way I am attracted by beggars and deserts, and from the insane fits of pity to which I am often a prey. All of these amount to various forms of renunciation. We carry in our blood the poisonous dregs of the absolute: it prevents us from breathing yet we cannot live without it.

Let God pray for the man in whom there is nothing left to die!

APPENDIX

Saints and Mystics mentioned in
Tears and Saints

ST. AGNES, martyr. Died c. 304. One of the most famous Roman martyrs. Her real story is shrouded in myth,
but she is said to have been a very young girl who refused to
marry and offered her maidenhood to God; she offered herself for martyrdom when persecution broke out in Rome,
was executed by a stab in the throat, and buried in the cemetery on the via Nomentana, where a church was built in her
honor c. 350. Her emblem is the lamb.

This appendix was compiled with information taken from *The Penguin Dictionary of
Saints*, ed. Donald Attwater (Middlesex, England: Penguin, 1965); *Le petit Larousse*
(Paris: Larousse, 1964); *A Biographical Dictionary of the Saints*, ed. F. G. Holweck (St.
Louis: B. Herder, 1924); Jacobus de Voragine, *The Golden Legend*, Granger Ryan and
Helmuth Ripperger, trans. (New York: Arno Press, 1969); *Dictionnaire de spiritualité
ascétique et mystique* (Paris: Beauchesne, 1990); *Rumi: Poet and Mystic*, trans. and with an
introduction by Reynold A. Nicholson (London: George Allen and Unwin, 1956);
The Ruins of the Heart: Selected Lyric Poetry of Jelaludin Rumi, trans. and with an
introduction by Edmund Helminski (London: Threshold Books, 1981).

ST. ALDEGUND, foundress of Maubeuge convent. Born c. 630 in Hainaut, Belgium, of the royal house of the Merovingians. Died in 685 of cancer. She is a patroness against cancer.

BLESSED ANGELA DA FOLIGNO, matron, penitent, mystical writer. Born 1248 of a noble family; died 1309. She married very young and led a dissipated life until the deaths of her husband, children, and mother, after which she joined the Third Order of St. Francis and did severe penance for her sins. Famous for her visions and revelations, she was called "Mistress of Theologians." She wrote a very popular book of her revelations.

ST. BRIDGET (Birgitta) of Sweden, foundress. Born in Sweden, c. 1303; died in Rome, 23 July 1373. A noblewoman who after her husband's death in 1344 founded the Order of the Holy Savior ("Brigettines") for women. She spent much time in Rome, living chastely and austerely, tending the sick and the poor. She claimed to have religious visions and dictated a book of "Revelations" which was both influential and controversial.

(ANN) CATHERINE EMMERICH, Augustinian nun, Germany, died 1824. She received the stigmata (marks resembling the five wounds of the crucified Jesus) and had visions. State and religious authorities fearing some kind of fraud, she became the object of a prolonged governmental, religious and scientific inquiry.

ST. CATHERINE OF GENOA, mystic. Born at Genoa, 1447; died there, 1510. At sixteen she made a marriage of convenience to a wealthy Genoan, an ill-tempered and unfaithful man. In 1473, she underwent a conversion. She was very devout, going to communion every day, and was prone to mystical trances. She managed to convert her husband,

and they both devoted their lives to caring for the sick to the point of risking their own lives. The essence of her religious thought is contained in her *Treatise on Purgatory* and *Spiritual Dialogue.*

ST. CATHERINE OF RICCI, visionary. Born at Florence, 1522; died at Prato, 1590. She was a nun and prioress of a Dominican convent in Prato, Tuscany. She had exceptional religious experiences, such as weekly ecstasies over a period of twelve years in which she relived Christ's passion. She was concerned with reform of the church, and revered the memory of Savonarola, who had been hanged and burned for heresy by Pope Alexander VI in 1498.

ST. CATHERINE OF SIENA, mystic. Born at Siena, 1347; died in Rome, 1380. She was the youngest daughter of a Sienese dyer. She resisted her parents's efforts to marry her and became a tertiary of the Dominican order, living at home, spending much time in prayer. She experienced many ecstasies, and received the stigmata, but without visible lesions. She was surrounded by converts known as the "Caterinati." Late in life, she became involved in public affairs, when she mediated between Florence and the papal government, helping to bring Pope Gregory XI back from Avignon to Rome. Her dictated *Dialogue* is an Italian classic.

CHEMS-EDDIN (Shamsu'l-Dîn of Tabriz). See Djelal-eddin-Rumi.

CHRISTINA EBNER, 1277–1356, originally from Nüremberg, she wrote in the tradition of "nuptial mysticism." (She is unrelated to her contemporary, the Dominican nun Marguerite Ebner).

ST. CUNEGUND, Holy Roman empress. Died 1033. She is reputed to have had a celibate marriage with her husband, Henry II of Bavaria. Both she and her husband were zealous supporters of Benedictine monasticism.

DIANA D'ANDOLO, thirteenth-century nun from Bologna. Abducted from the convent by her parents, she returned to the community and founded the convent of St. Agnes.

DIODATA DEGLI ADEMARI, unidentified.

DJELAL-EDDIN-RUMI (Jalalu'l-Dîn Rūmi; Jeláludin Rumi), the greatest mystical poet of Persia. Born in the province of Khorasan in 1207; died in Konia (Turkey) in 1273. Rumi's work is a synthesis of Arab, Hellenistic, Hermetic, Christian, Jewish, Indian, and Persian sources. He propounded a religion of love. Two of his most famous works, *Diwan-i Shams-i Tabriz* ("The Poems of Shams of Tabriz") and the epic *Mathnawi* ("The Book of Hussam"), were inspired by his Platonic love for the "Perfect Man," i.e., a man in whom divine qualities are revealed, and whom the lover sees as his alter ego. Rumi's mystical relation to Chemseddin of Tabriz is a fascinating love story. According to the legend, Rumi met a vagrant dervish or holy man who asked him a question that made him faint. He then answered the question, and took the man into his house. For two years they were inseparable, steeped in mystical intercourse, and forgetful of the rest of the world. Rumi's neglected disciples grew jealous and chased Chems-eddin away to Damascus. He came back, however, at Rumi's entreaties, but after a while mysteriously disappeared. He may have been murdered by jealous disciples, or he may have gone away for good. Rumi was overcome by passionate grief, and invented the "whirling dervish" dance as an expression of his powerful emotion. At the plaintive sound of a reed flute, he would dance himself into a trance, and compose poetry which his disciples jotted down. The mystical love poems thus composed were collected into the *Diwan,* written in the name of the lost lover and dedicated to him.

DOROTHEA OF MONTAU, pious widow, born in East Prussia 1347; died 1394. She was married against her will to an armorer, a mean-spirited man by whom she had nine children. Her married life was full of grim austerity: she would bind sharp nut shells around her loins or place them in open wounds so that she wouldn't enjoy intercourse, and she would burn her nipples so that she wouldn't derive pleasure from nursing. After her husband's death, she had herself walled up in a cell at the Cathedral of Marienweder. She possessed mystical gifts.

ECKHART, JOHANN, known as MEISTER ECKHART, German mystic, c. 1260–1327. A Dominican monk, he was a disciple of Thomas Aquinas. A preacher and spiritual guide in religious and beguine communities, he was accused of unorthodox views, and his theories were condemned by the pope.

ST. FRANCIS OF ASSISI, founder of the Friars Minor. Born at Assisi, c. 1181; died in the chapel of the Portiuncula, 1226. Son of a wealthy merchant, he led an easy life as a young man until sickness and the experience of war sobered him up. While praying in the church of San Damiano one day, he had a vision of Christ who urged him: "Francis, repair my fallen house!" He took the words literally, raising money for the repairs of the church by selling goods from his father's house. He was disinherited, and started the poor life of a roving preacher. Along with eleven other men, he founded the order of the Friars Minor, known for their simplicity and humility. In 1224, while praying in the Apennines, he received the stigmata (Christ's five wounds at the crucifixion) which he kept until his death.

ST. FRANCIS DE SALES, bishop and writer. Born at Annecy, 1567; died at Lyons, 1622. Son of a nobleman, he was ordained priest against his father's wishes. He was sent to convert the people of his native Chablais country from Calvinism to Roman Catholicism. Bishop of Geneva, founder, with Jane de Chantel, of the Order of the Visitation. His most famous book, *The Love of God*, is the story of the love for God in ordinary men's hearts and lives.

ST. IGNATIUS OF LOYOLA, founder of the Society of Jesus. Born at Loyola, Spain, c. 1491; died in Rome, 1556. He was the youngest son of an ancient noble Basque family. Lived first as a soldier, was wounded at the battle of Pamplona, and during a long convalescence read the lives of Christ and the saints, and decided to dedicate himself to God. The Society of Jesus was organized as a regular religious order but with one additional vow, that of being at the pope's disposal anywhere, anytime: it is very active in the missionary and educational fields. St. Ignatius was prone to religious illuminations and left a famous book, *Spiritual Exercises*, which instructs readers in the steps that help to produce visions or states of profound meditation.

ST. JOHN OF THE CROSS, mystical theologian and poet. Born near Avila 1542; died at Ubeda, 1591. Son of an impoverished noble family, he became a Carmelite friar. He met Teresa of Avila, and joined the first of the reformed houses for men in the order. For his reform work, he was imprisoned at Toledo by the Carmelite prior general, and there he wrote his first poems. His chief works are poems with corresponding commentaries: *The Dark Night of the Soul, The Spiritual Canticle, The Living Flame of Love.*

MARGARET OF CORTONA, born at Laviano, 1247; died at Cortona, 1297. The beautiful daughter of Tuscan peasants, she was the mistress of a young nobleman to whom she bore a son. After her lover's violent death, she was given refuge in a friend's house in Cortona. She became a Franciscan tertiary, leading an austere and devout life of hardwork and charity. She converted many sinners, and her confessor, Friar Giunta, recorded her supernatural revelations.

ST. MARGARET MARY ALACOQUE, born in Burgundy, 1647; died at Paray-le-Monial, 1690. She was the daughter of a notary, Claud Alacoque, and entered the Visitation convent at Paray-le-Monial after an unhappy and sickly childhood. She had four visitations from Jesus Christ concerning devotion towards his heart, symbol of his love for mankind. She suffered persecution at the hands of the other nuns, who accused her of having delusions. She became very influential among Roman Catholics after the Feast of the Sacred Heart was made official in 1856.

MARIANNA OF QUITO, Ecuador, died 1645. Also known as St. Mariana Paredes y Flores. South American girl who tended the poor and taught Indian children in her home. She undertook harsh penitential practices, and during an epidemic in Quito she offered her life in expiation for the sins of others. She died soon after.

ST. MARTHA, first century. The sister of Lazarus and Mary of Bethany. She served Jesus, and is a patroness of those helping the poor. It was to her that Jesus declared: "I am the resurrection and the life. . . . "

ST. MARY MAGDALEN DE PAZZI, mystic. Born at Florence, 1566; died there, 1607. A Carmelite nun at seventeen, suffered inner doubts, followed by great spiritual consolations. Made prayer and penance her vocation.

ST. MARY MAGDALENE. (The same person as Mary of Bethany according to a Western tradition). First century. Mary of Magdala, healed by Jesus of the "seven evils," followed him into Galilee and was present at the crucifixion. With two others, she went and found the empty tomb. According to Mark, Christ first showed himself to her. John adds that she was given a message for the brethren.

ST. MECHTHILD OF MAGDEBURG, thirteenth century. German beguine and mystical writer associated with the monastery of Helfta, Germany. The beguines were women who lived poor, austere, chaste, and charitable lives apart from the world but who did not take vows, and had no hierarchy of officials or powerful and wealthy leaders. Their counterparts in Southern Europe are the tertiaries, women who were loosely connected with one of the great mendicant orders, Franciscan and Dominican.

MEZZI SIDWIBRIN, unidentified.

ST. PETER OF ALCÁNTARA, mystic. Born in Alcantara, Spain, 1499; died at Arenas, 1562. Reformer of the Franciscan order: the friars lived in great poverty, going barefoot, spending much time in solitude and contemplation. Confessor to St. Teresa of Avila, he helped her found the first convent of reformed Carmelite nuns. Greatest Spanish mystic before St. Teresa, he wrote a *Treatise on Prayer and Meditation.*

PLOTINUS, Neo-Platonic philosopher. Born into a Roman family established in Egypt (204–70 A.D.). His philosophy mixed pagan and Christian doctrines.

RANCÉ, ARMAND DE, abbé, reformer of the Order of Trappists. Born and died in Paris (1626–1700).

ST. ROSE OF LIMA, recluse. Born in Lima, Peru (1586–1671). Isabel de Flores y del Oliva, known as Rose, she was the first Latin American to be canonized. She refused to marry and became a Dominican tertiary, earning a livelihood for herself and her family by growing flowers and doing embroidery work. The cruel penances she inflicted on herself and her mystical experiences were criticized by her family and became the object of ecclesiastical inquiry. She tended the poor and the Indians and is the originator of social services in Peru.

HENRY SUSO (Henrich Seuse), called "Amandus," German mystic. Born 1295 of a noble family; died 1366. He joined the Dominican order at Cologne where he studied under Eckhart. He had frequent visions, and led a life of austerity. He wrote the *Little Book of Eternal Wisdom*, a gem of German mysticism.

ST. TERESA OF AVILA, foundress and mystic. Born in Avila, Spain, 1515; died at Alba de Tormes, 1582. With Catherine of Siena, one of the first two women to be declared doctors of the Church, in 1970. She became a Carmelite nun at twenty, and suffered from serious ill-health. She spent much time in contemplation and was prone to mystical ecstasy. Among her spiritual experiences was the piercing of her heart by a spear of divine love. In spite of her poor health, she combined a life of contemplation with intense activity, and founded convents under the original strict form of the Carmelite rule. Her nuns were known as *descalzas* ("barefooted"). Her most important writings are the *Life*, written at the request of her confessors, *The Way of Perfection*, an instruction manual for her nuns, *The Book of Foundations*, and *The Interior Castle.*

ST. THÉRÈSE OF LISIEUX, Carmelite nun (1873–1897). She led an uneventful life as a nun until she became ill with tuberculosis and died after much suffering at twenty-four. Two years before her death, she was told to write her recollections of childhood, to which she added an account of her life. After her death, the book was published under the title *Histoire d'une âme* (*The Story of a Soul*) and was widely read, making her the most popular nun of modern times.

ST. THOMAS AQUINAS, theologian (1225–1274). Son of a Lombard nobleman, he joined the Dominican order and became a mendicant friar. His decision shocked his family, who kidnapped him and imprisoned him for a year. On his release he went to Paris and Cologne, and in 1256 took his master's degree in theology. His most famous and influential works are *Summa contra Gentiles,* a treatise on God, and *Summa theologiae,* a systematic exposition of theology. He left the latter unfinished, declaring: "All I have written seems to me like straw compared with what I have seen and what has been revealed to me."